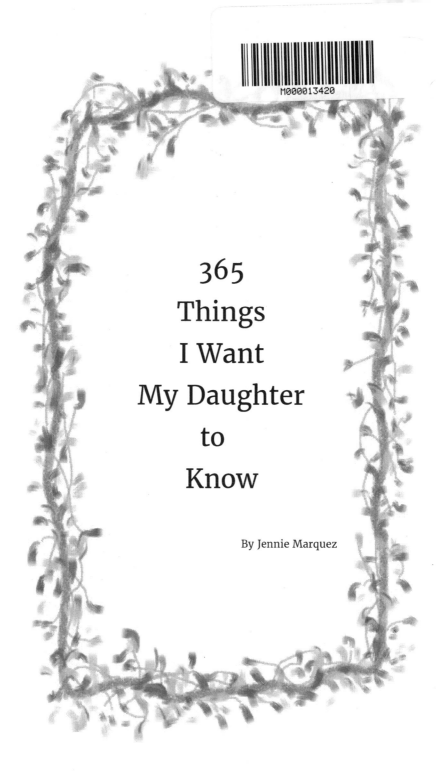

365
Things
I Want
My Daughter
to
Know

By Jennie Marquez

Cover designed by Jennie N. Marquez

Jennie N. Marquez

Printed in the United States of America

First Printing: Dec 2018

ISBN-9781790534401

You have gone up & down many hills, But nothing in this life will stop you from climbing to the top but You! When you feel the challenges are too tough remember, nothing is tougher than your will to be your personal Best & my love for You!

For Alex,
   The most unbelievable girl
   All my love!!!
      Mom

I am so proud of your Journey! ♡ Thank you! Love Mom -2019-

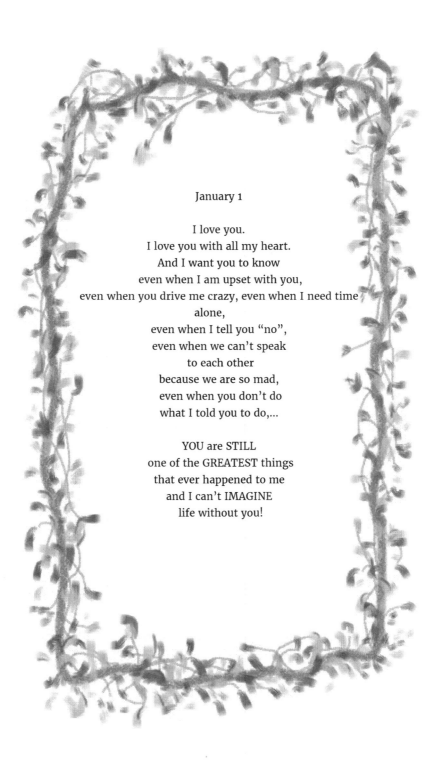

January 1

I love you.
I love you with all my heart.
And I want you to know
even when I am upset with you,
even when you drive me crazy, even when I need time
alone,
even when I tell you "no",
even when we can't speak
to each other
because we are so mad,
even when you don't do
what I told you to do,...

YOU are STILL
one of the GREATEST things
that ever happened to me
and I can't IMAGINE
life without you!

January 2

Being a teen-age girl is sometimes hard
and often times confusing.
It is a time when you start
to figure out who you are
and who you want to be.
It may seem like if you make a decision and it's not the
"Right" one,
your life will be ruined.
DON'T WORRY!
You are not going to make
ALL the right decisions.
MOST of them will not be totally right.
But that is not a path for ruining your life.

It's a path for DISCOVERING your life,
for LEARNING what is Right for YOU!
You are going to figure out the right path for you,
one mistake at a time.

Enjoy the Journey!

January 3

Boys come and go.
In fact, people in your life
come and go.
Mostly you won't notice.
But when you do notice
that someone is leaving your life, it's sad.
It's okay to be sad.
Just know that this
is how it was meant to be.
We all only have so much time
in our lives.
If some people do not leave
our lives,
we do not have room to add others.
So, when it is time for someone to go, remember
you were blessed to have them in your life for the period that
you did,
and now it is time
to be blessed
by someone else's presence
in your life.

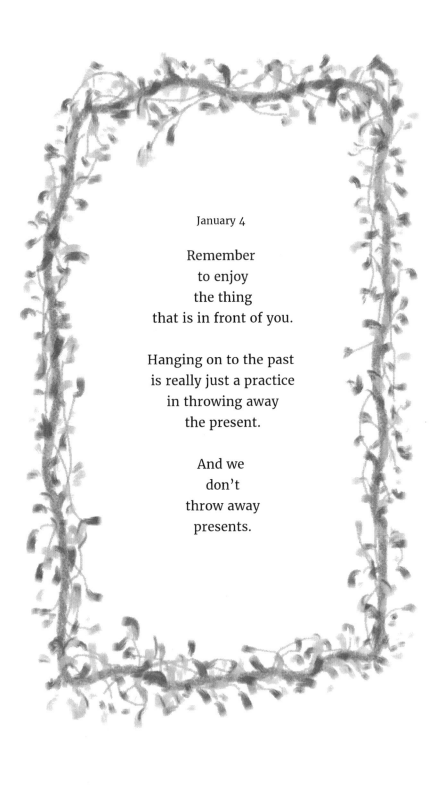

January 4

Remember
to enjoy
the thing
that is in front of you.

Hanging on to the past
is really just a practice
in throwing away
the present.

And we
don't
throw away
presents.

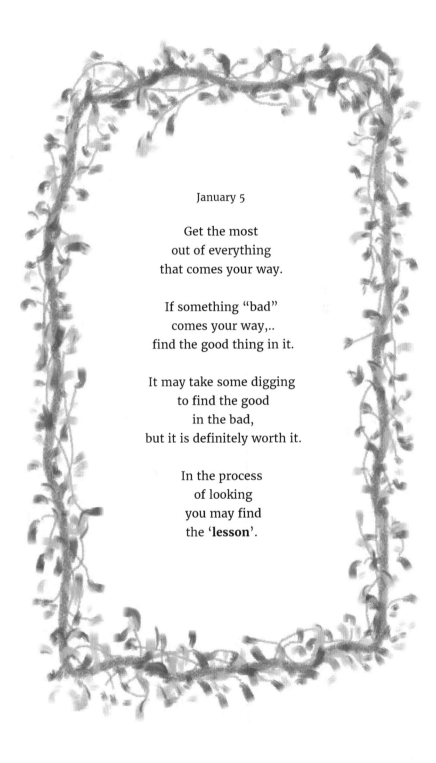

January 5

Get the most
out of everything
that comes your way.

If something "bad"
comes your way,..
find the good thing in it.

It may take some digging
to find the good
in the bad,
but it is definitely worth it.

In the process
of looking
you may find
the '**lesson**'.

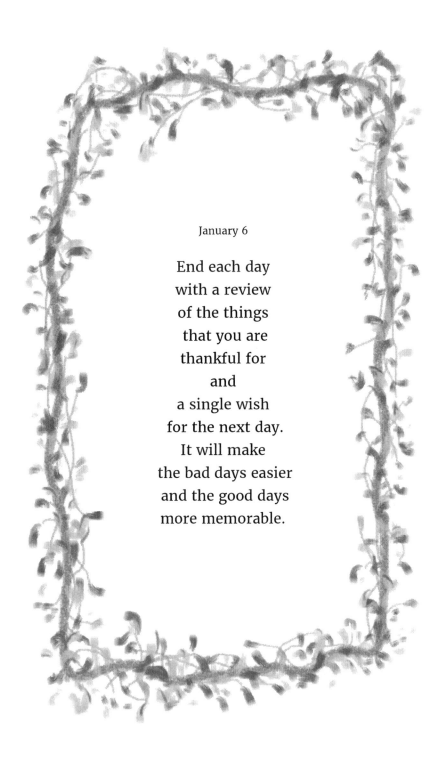

January 6

End each day
with a review
of the things
that you are
thankful for
and
a single wish
for the next day.
It will make
the bad days easier
and the good days
more memorable.

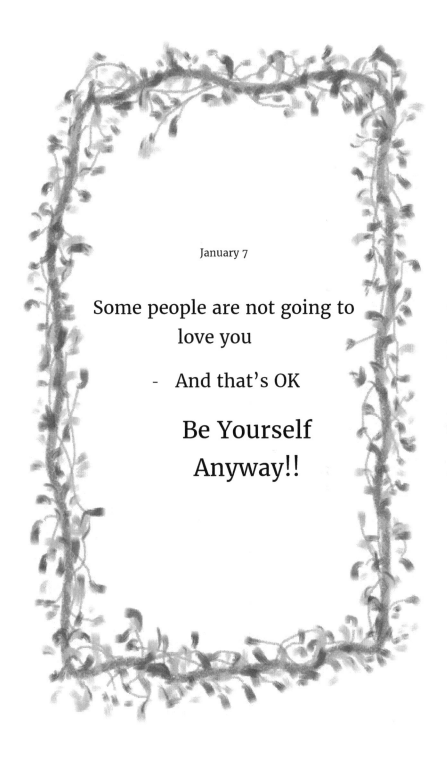

January 7

Some people are not going to love you

\- And that's OK

Be Yourself
Anyway!!

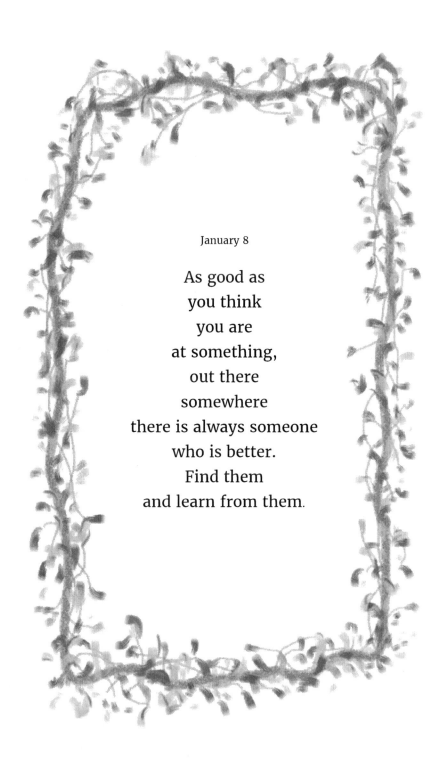

January 8

As good as
you think
you are
at something,
out there
somewhere
there is always someone
who is better.
Find them
and learn from them.

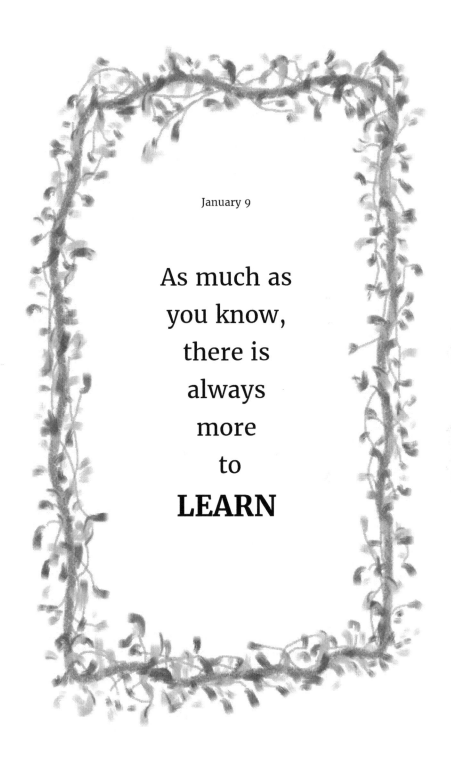

January 9

As much as
you know,
there is
always
more
to
LEARN

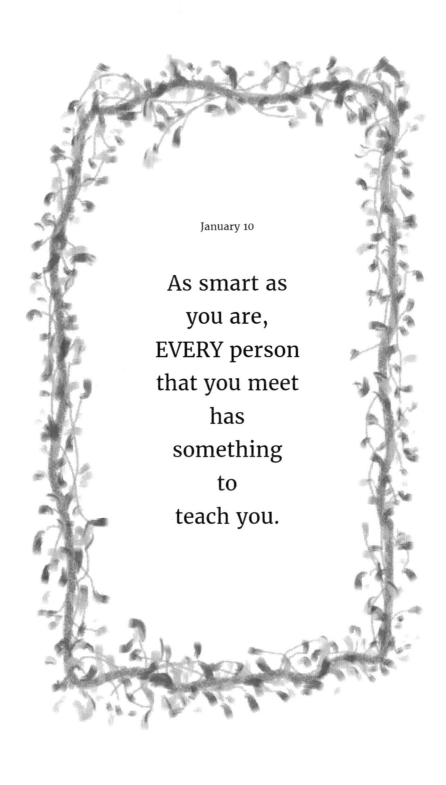

January 10

As smart as
you are,
EVERY person
that you meet
has
something
to
teach you.

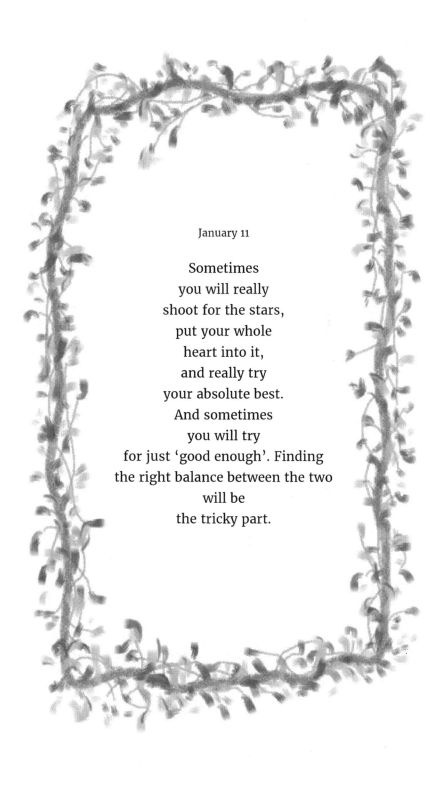

January 11

Sometimes
you will really
shoot for the stars,
put your whole
heart into it,
and really try
your absolute best.
And sometimes
you will try
for just 'good enough'. Finding
the right balance between the two
will be
the tricky part.

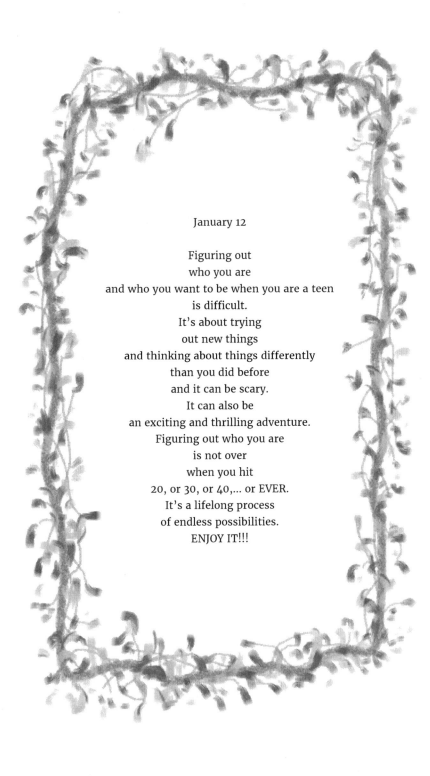

January 12

Figuring out
who you are
and who you want to be when you are a teen
is difficult.
It's about trying
out new things
and thinking about things differently
than you did before
and it can be scary.
It can also be
an exciting and thrilling adventure.
Figuring out who you are
is not over
when you hit
20, or 30, or 40,... or EVER.
It's a lifelong process
of endless possibilities.
ENJOY IT!!!

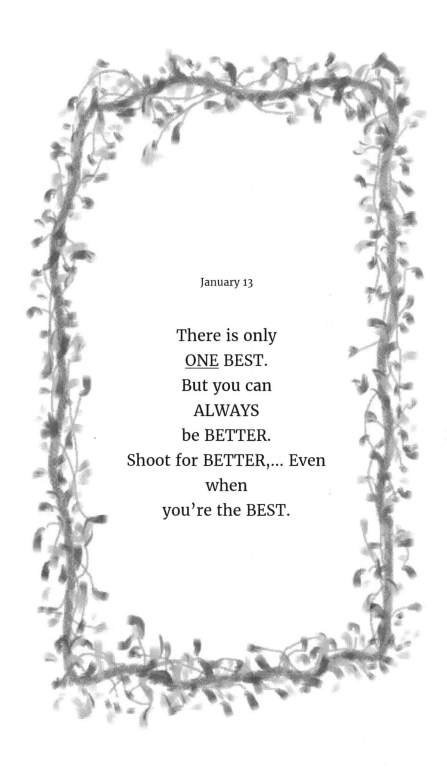

January 13

There is only
<u>ONE</u> BEST.
But you can
ALWAYS
be BETTER.
Shoot for BETTER,... Even
when
you're the BEST.

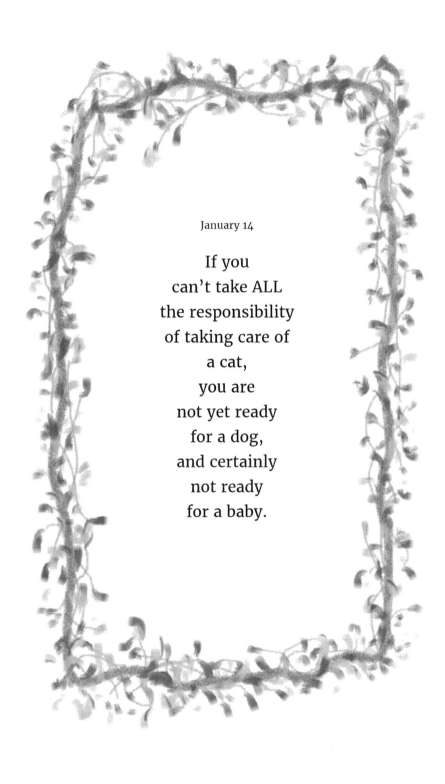

January 14

If you
can't take ALL
the responsibility
of taking care of
a cat,
you are
not yet ready
for a dog,
and certainly
not ready
for a baby.

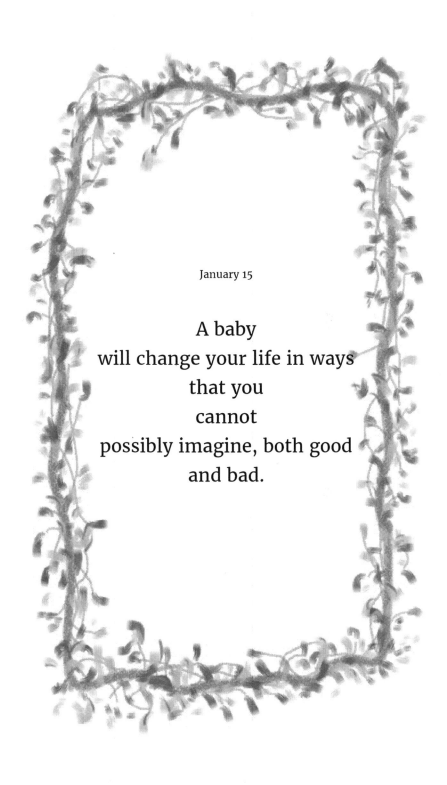

January 15

A baby
will change your life in ways
that you
cannot
possibly imagine, both good
and bad.

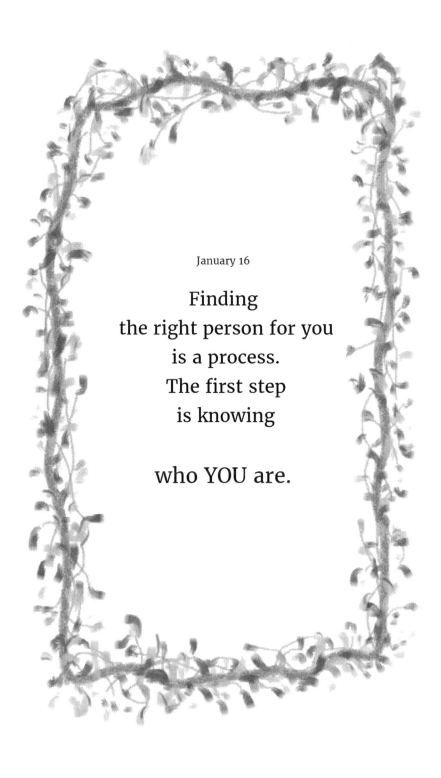

January 16

Finding
the right person for you
is a process.
The first step
is knowing

who YOU are.

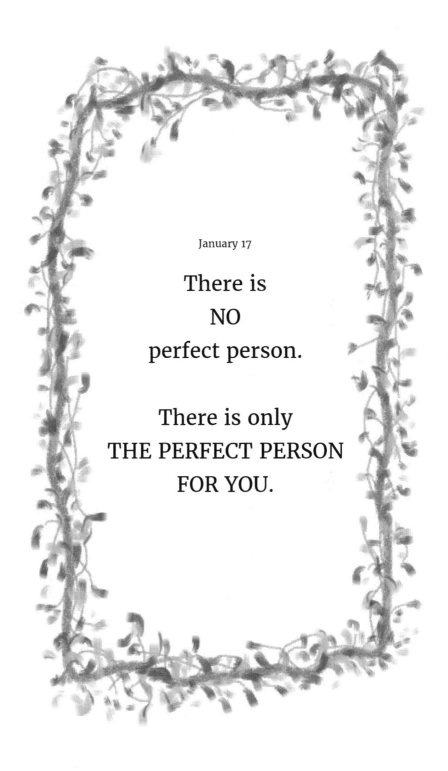

January 17

There is
NO
perfect person.

There is only
THE PERFECT PERSON
FOR YOU.

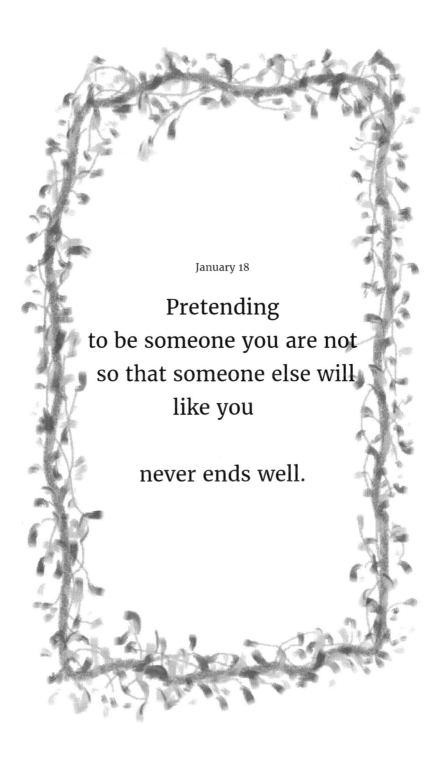

January 18

Pretending
to be someone you are not
so that someone else will
like you

never ends well.

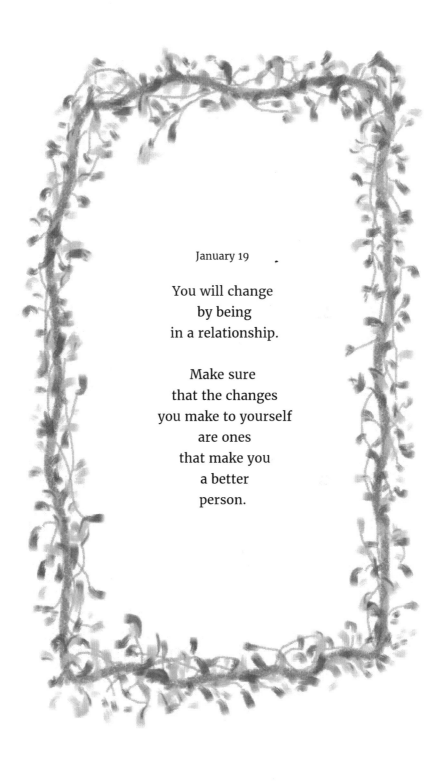

January 19

You will change
by being
in a relationship.

Make sure
that the changes
you make to yourself
are ones
that make you
a better
person.

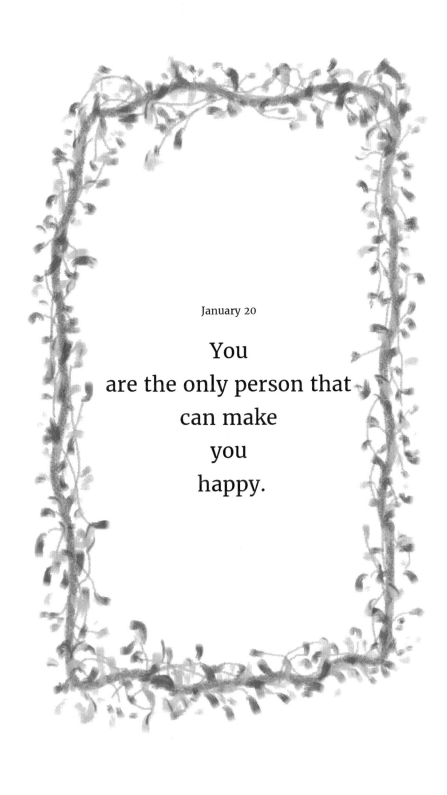

January 20

You
are the only person that
can make
you
happy.

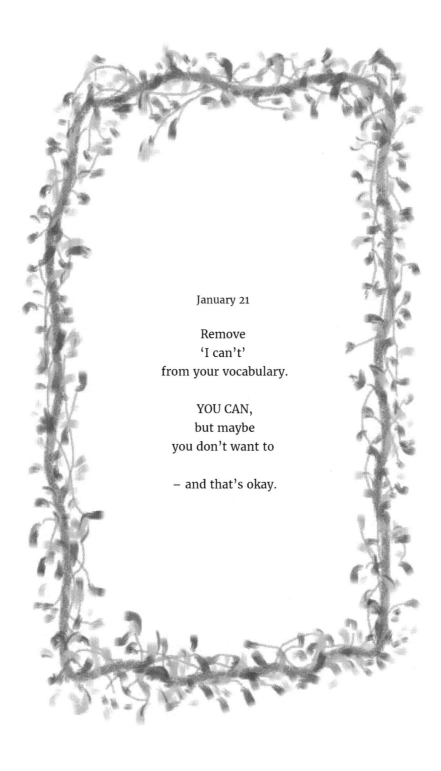

January 21

Remove
'I can't'
from your vocabulary.

YOU CAN,
but maybe
you don't want to

– and that's okay.

January 22

When you were born you relied on me to make your
life whatever it was, to keep you safe, to keep you healthy,
to keep you active, to teach you about life, to keep you
entertained, to make your choices for you,...

And, as you have grown, these things have slowly
shifted to your responsibility as you were ready for them.

And even when you are 'BIG' and all these
responsibilities lay firmly on your shoulders, KNOW that I
will ALWAYS be here to be your safety net and sounding
board until I need you to do that for me.

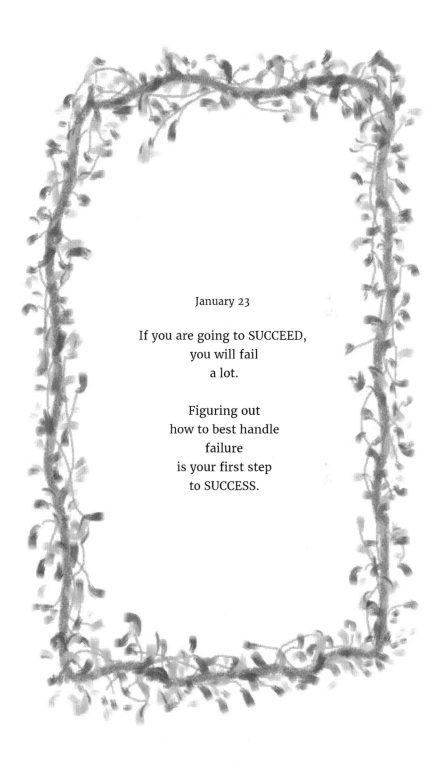

January 23

If you are going to SUCCEED,
you will fail
a lot.

Figuring out
how to best handle
failure
is your first step
to SUCCESS.

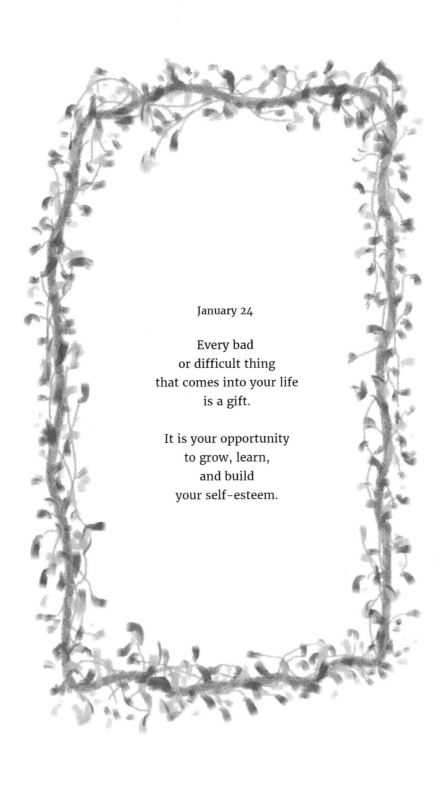

January 24

Every bad
or difficult thing
that comes into your life
is a gift.

It is your opportunity
to grow, learn,
and build
your self-esteem.

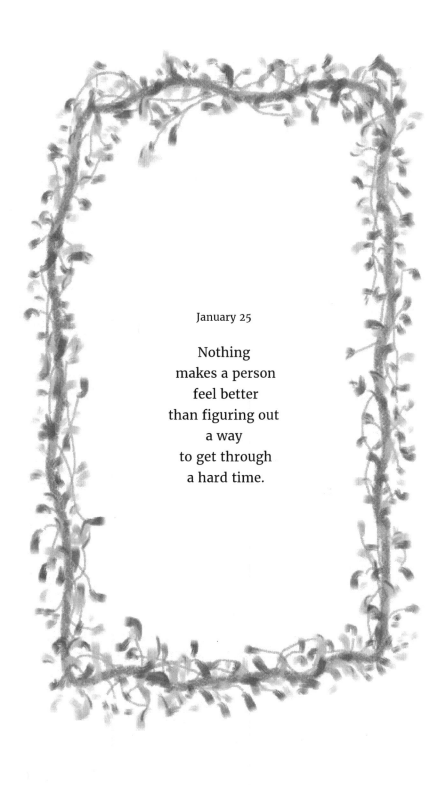

January 25

Nothing
makes a person
feel better
than figuring out
a way
to get through
a hard time.

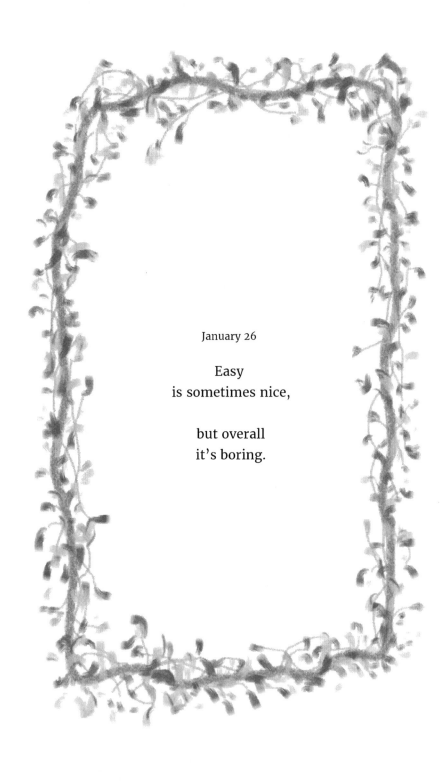

January 26

Easy
is sometimes nice,

but overall
it's boring.

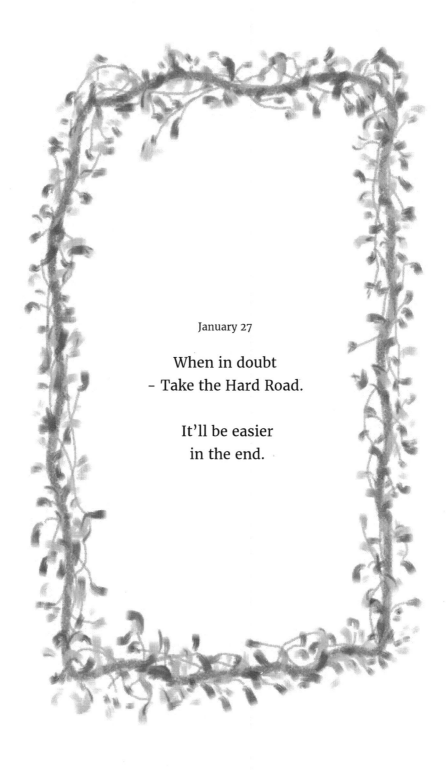

January 27

When in doubt
- Take the Hard Road.

It'll be easier
in the end.

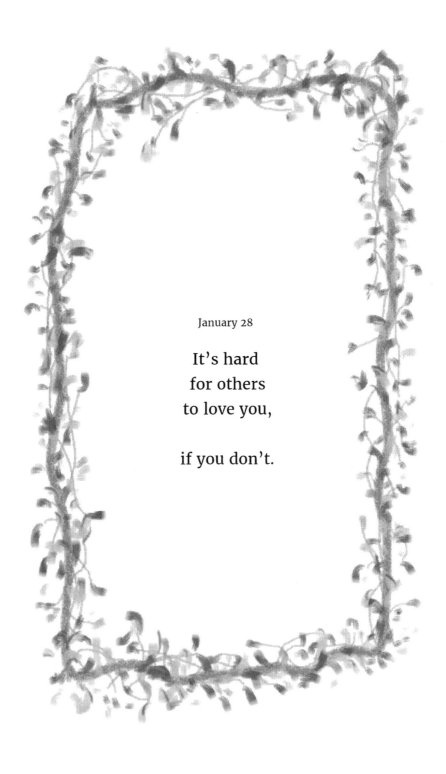

January 28

**It's hard
for others
to love you,**

if you don't.

January 29

Know
what you stand for
and
what you will
and won't put up with.

Of course,
this is a process,
so it changes
with time.

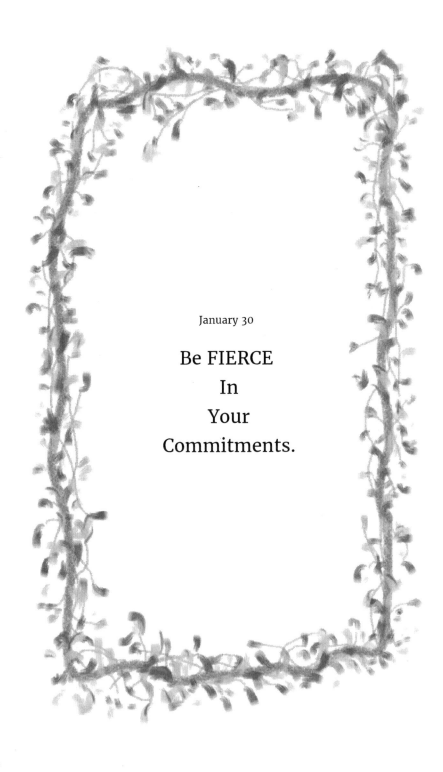

January 30

Be FIERCE
In
Your
Commitments.

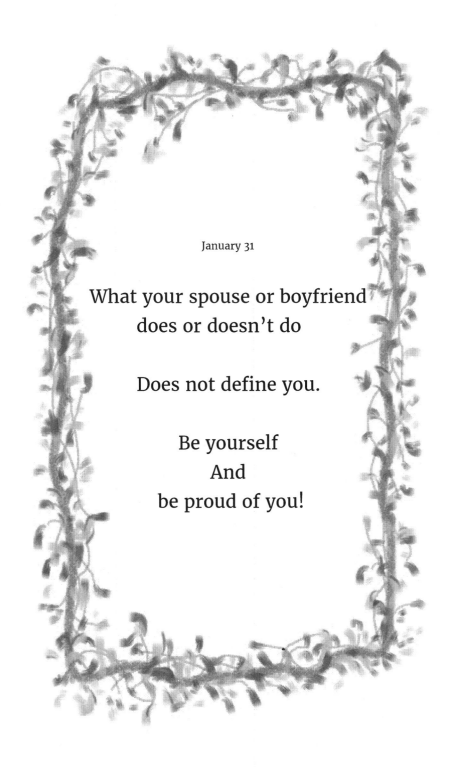

January 31

What your spouse or boyfriend
does or doesn't do

Does not define you.

Be yourself
And
be proud of you!

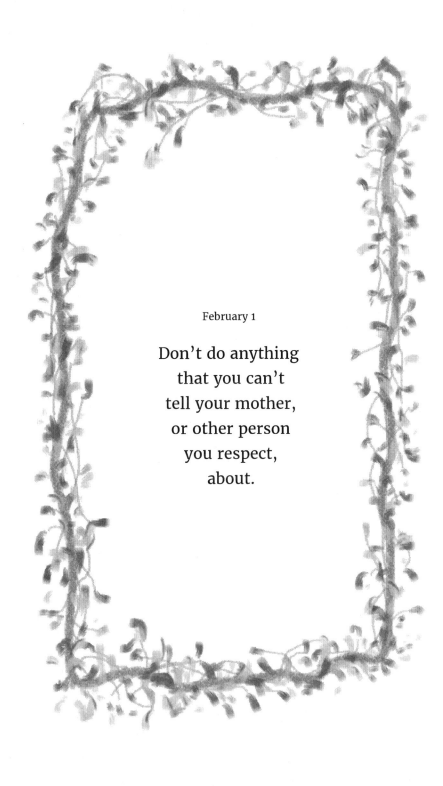

February 1

Don't do anything
that you can't
tell your mother,
or other person
you respect,
about.

February 2

If you are
not 'yourself'
when you are with others,
it can leave you
feeling empty.

Because
if they
don't REALLY KNOW you,... How
can they
REALLY LOVE you?

Be yourself!!

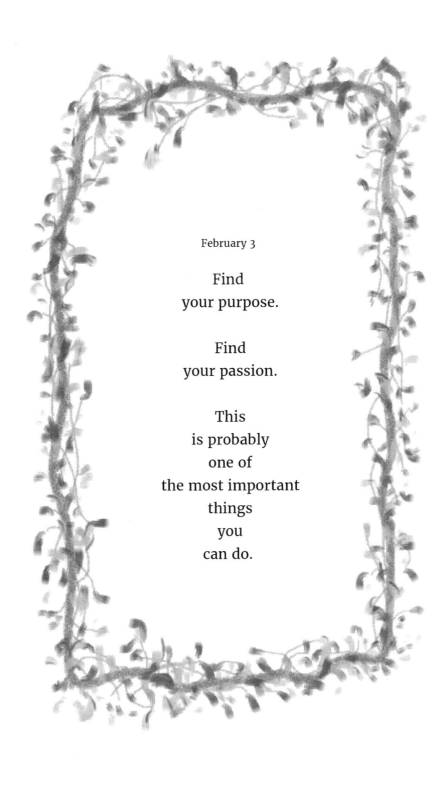

February 3

Find
your purpose.

Find
your passion.

This
is probably
one of
the most important
things
you
can do.

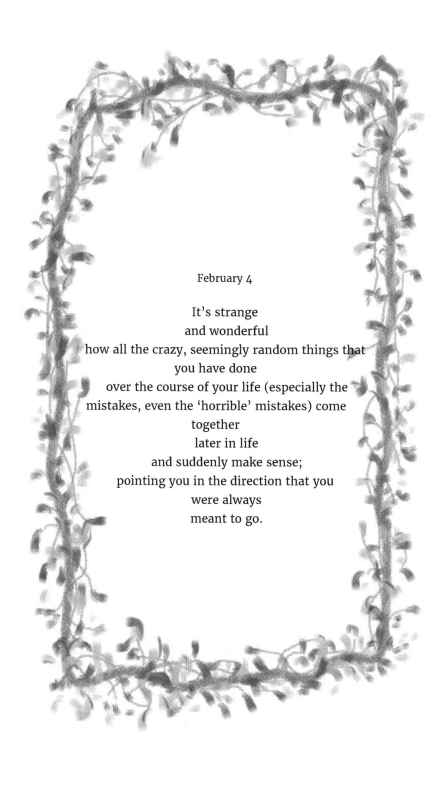

February 4

It's strange
and wonderful
how all the crazy, seemingly random things that
you have done
over the course of your life (especially the
mistakes, even the 'horrible' mistakes) come
together
later in life
and suddenly make sense;
pointing you in the direction that you
were always
meant to go.

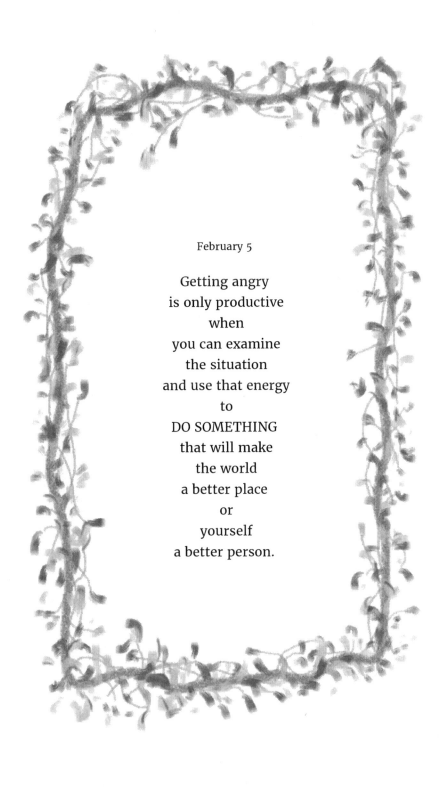

February 5

Getting angry
is only productive
when
you can examine
the situation
and use that energy
to
DO SOMETHING
that will make
the world
a better place
or
yourself
a better person.

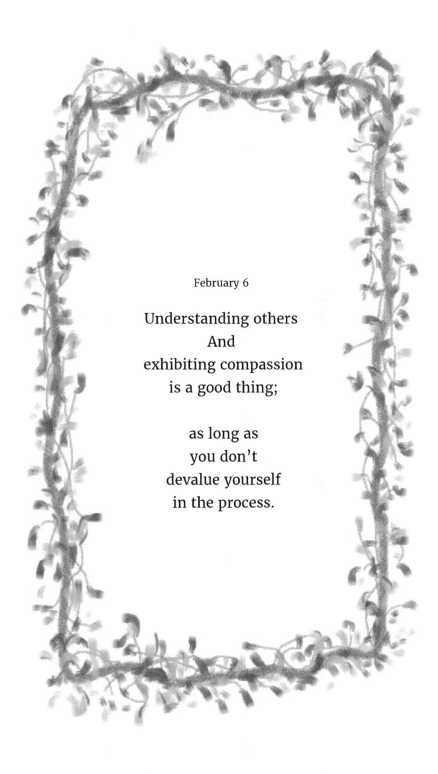

February 6

Understanding others
And
exhibiting compassion
is a good thing;

as long as
you don't
devalue yourself
in the process.

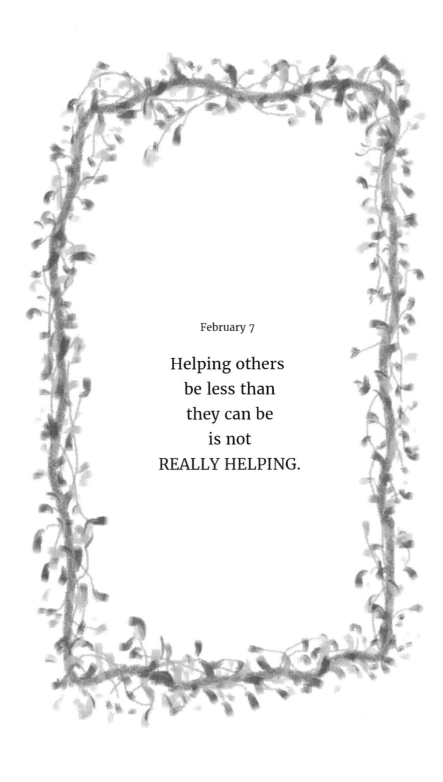

February 7

Helping others
be less than
they can be
is not
REALLY HELPING.

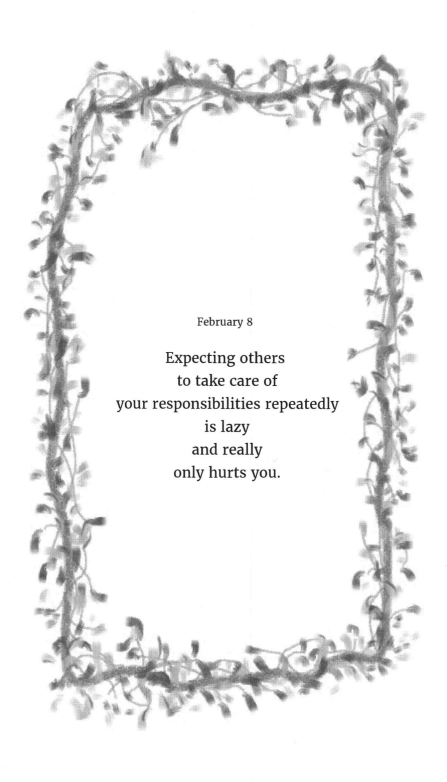

February 8

Expecting others
to take care of
your responsibilities repeatedly
is lazy
and really
only hurts you.

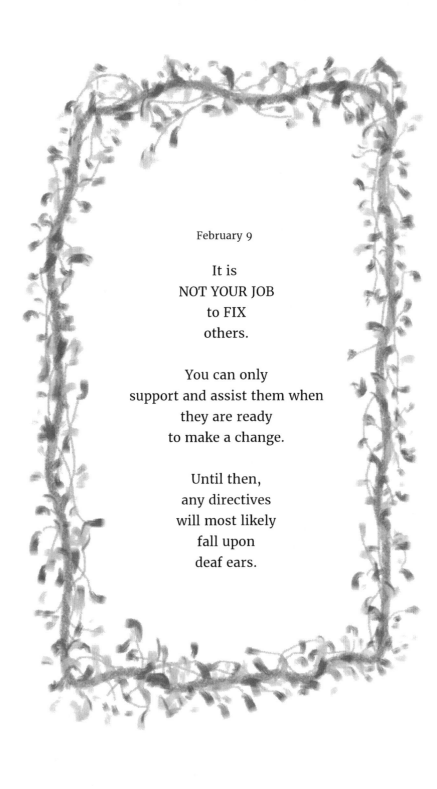

February 9

It is
NOT YOUR JOB
to FIX
others.

You can only
support and assist them when
they are ready
to make a change.

Until then,
any directives
will most likely
fall upon
deaf ears.

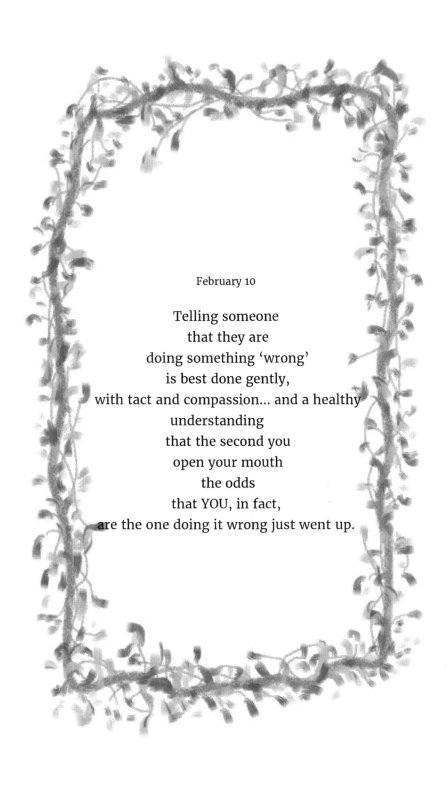

February 10

Telling someone
that they are
doing something 'wrong'
is best done gently,
with tact and compassion... and a healthy
understanding
that the second you
open your mouth
the odds
that YOU, in fact,
are the one doing it wrong just went up.

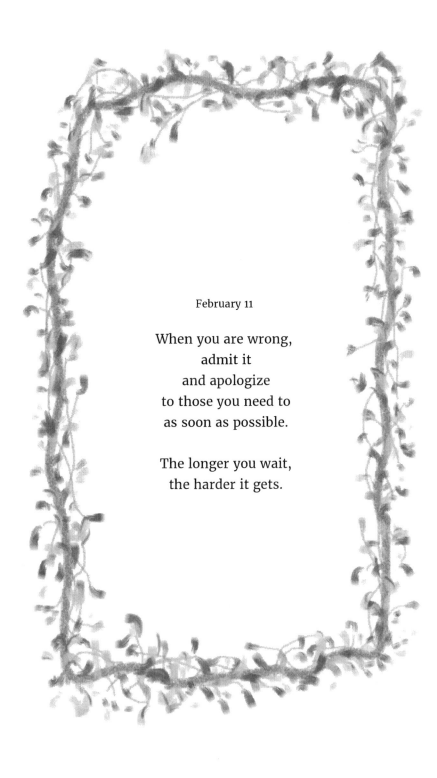

February 11

When you are wrong,
admit it
and apologize
to those you need to
as soon as possible.

The longer you wait,
the harder it gets.

February 12

Don't tell people
'what they want to hear'.

It belittles them
and makes you a liar.

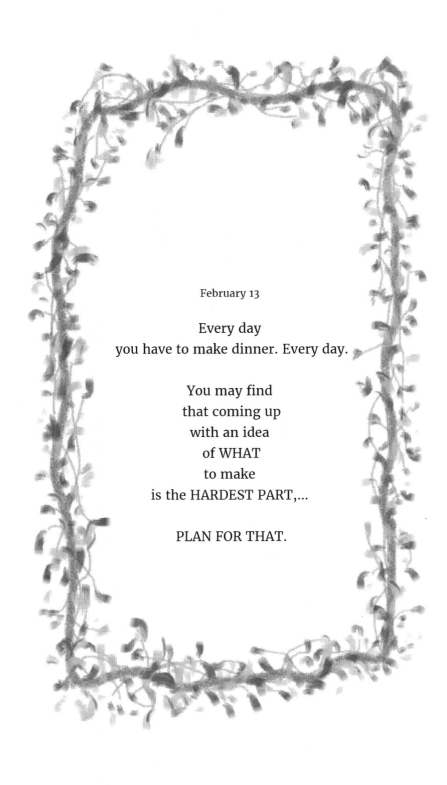

February 13

Every day
you have to make dinner. Every day.

You may find
that coming up
with an idea
of WHAT
to make
is the HARDEST PART,...

PLAN FOR THAT.

February 14

When things
seem overwhelming
and you start
to get down,
discouraged,
and unmotivated,

it may seem hard
to DO ANYTHING.

It's often easier
if you break it down
into smaller pieces

and then
DO ANYTHING.

February 15

Getting organized
gives you more time.

If you feel
you don't
have enough time,

spend
a little time
getting organized.

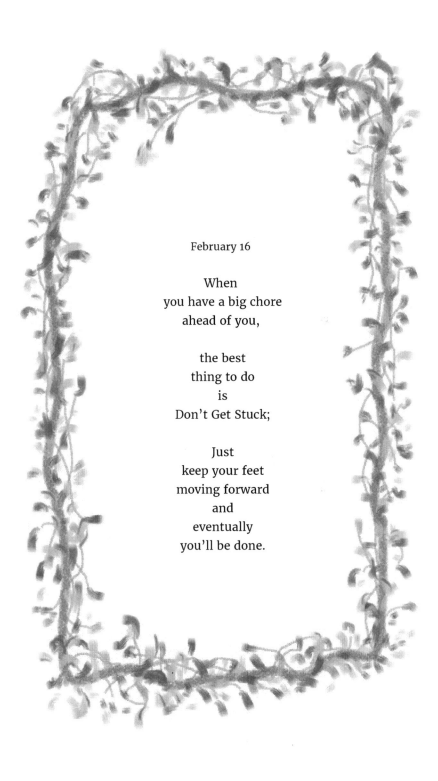

February 16

When
you have a big chore
ahead of you,

the best
thing to do
is
Don't Get Stuck;

Just
keep your feet
moving forward
and
eventually
you'll be done.

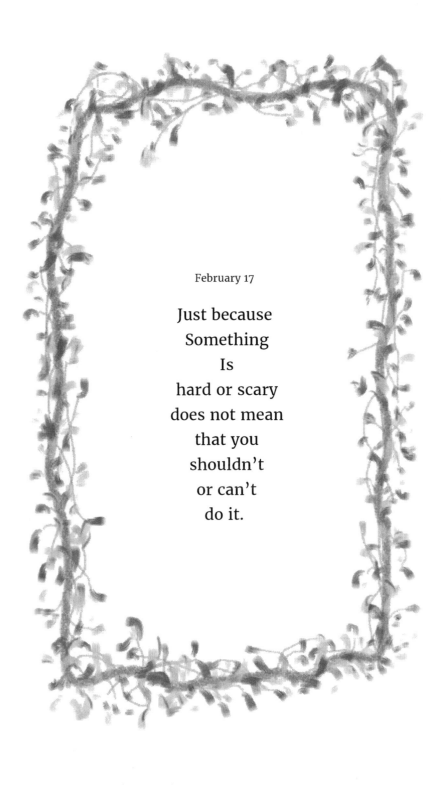

February 17

Just because
Something
Is
hard or scary
does not mean
that you
shouldn't
or can't
do it.

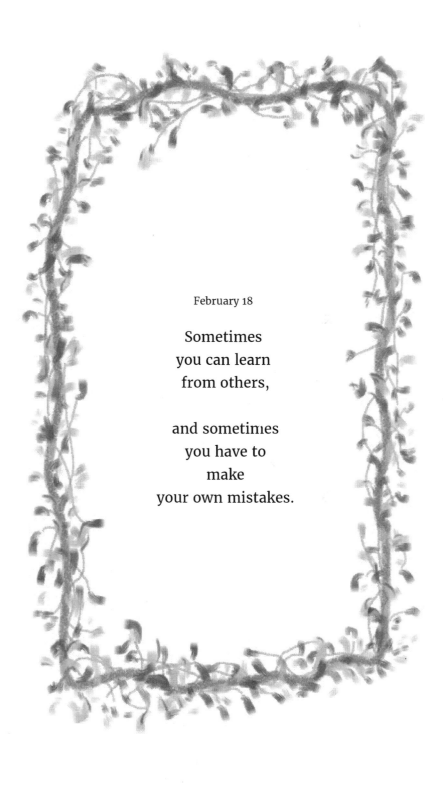

February 18

Sometimes
you can learn
from others,

and sometimes
you have to
make
your own mistakes.

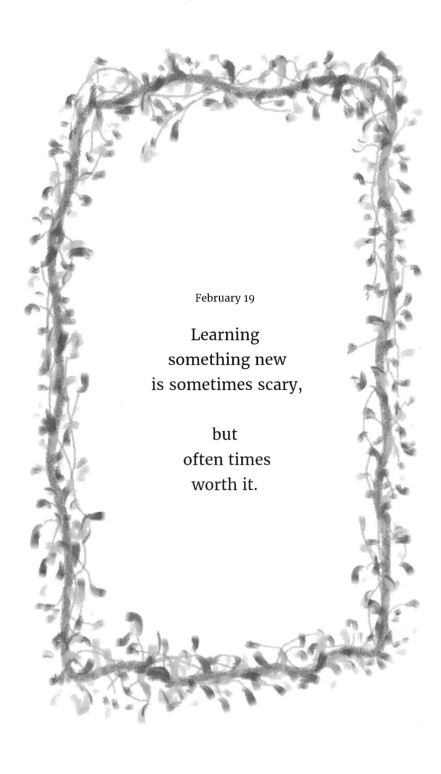

February 19

Learning
something new
is sometimes scary,

but
often times
worth it.

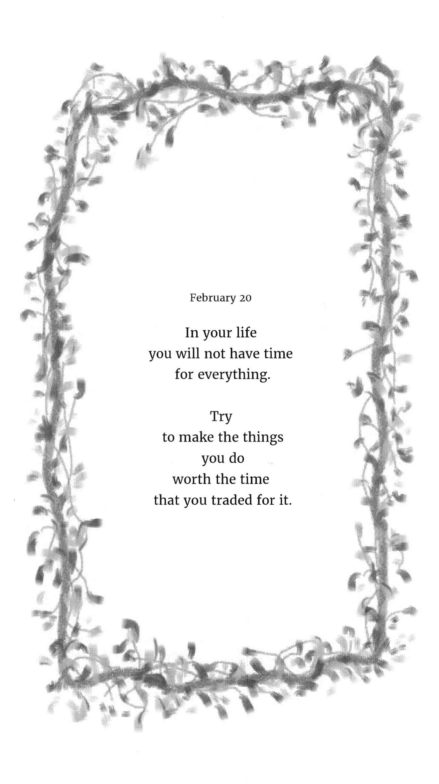

February 20

In your life
you will not have time
for everything.

Try
to make the things
you do
worth the time
that you traded for it.

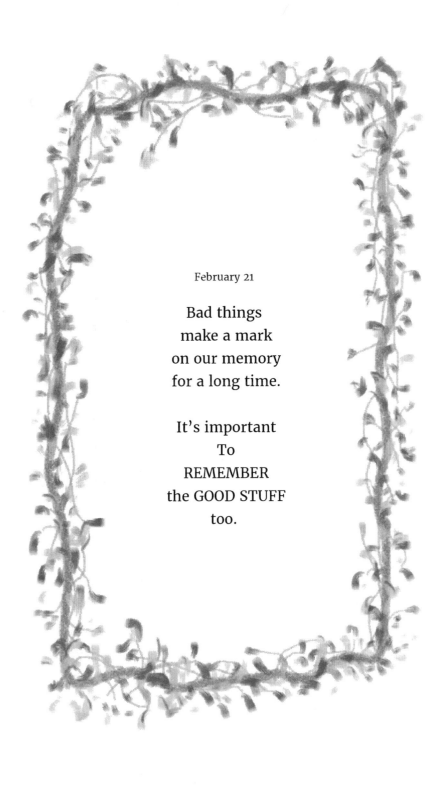

February 21

Bad things
make a mark
on our memory
for a long time.

It's important
To
REMEMBER
the GOOD STUFF
too.

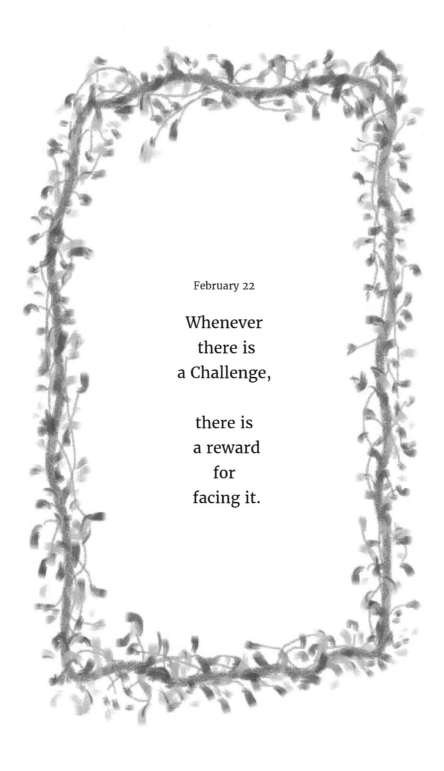

February 22

Whenever
there is
a Challenge,

there is
a reward
for
facing it.

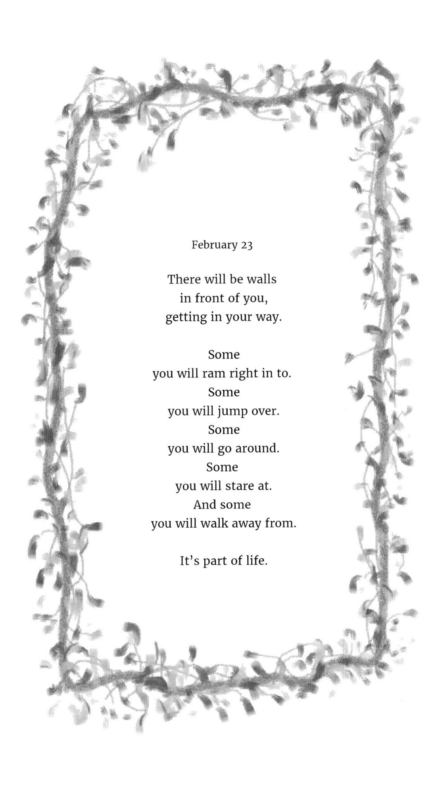

February 23

There will be walls
in front of you,
getting in your way.

Some
you will ram right in to.
Some
you will jump over.
Some
you will go around.
Some
you will stare at.
And some
you will walk away from.

It's part of life.

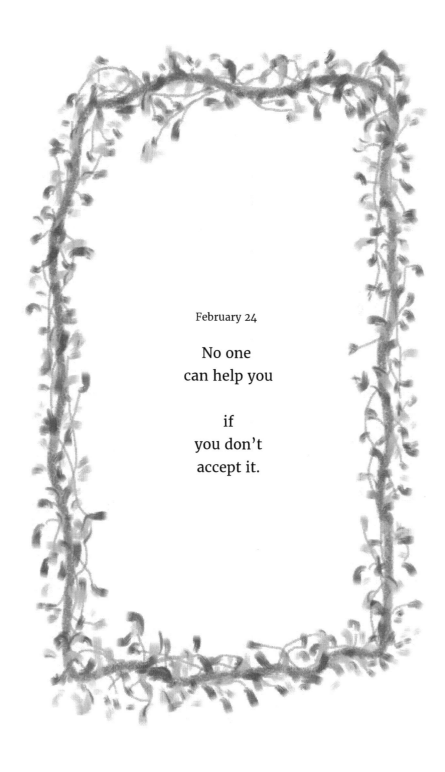

February 24

No one
can help you

if
you don't
accept it.

February 25

**Life
is only
as good
or
as bad
as you think it is.**

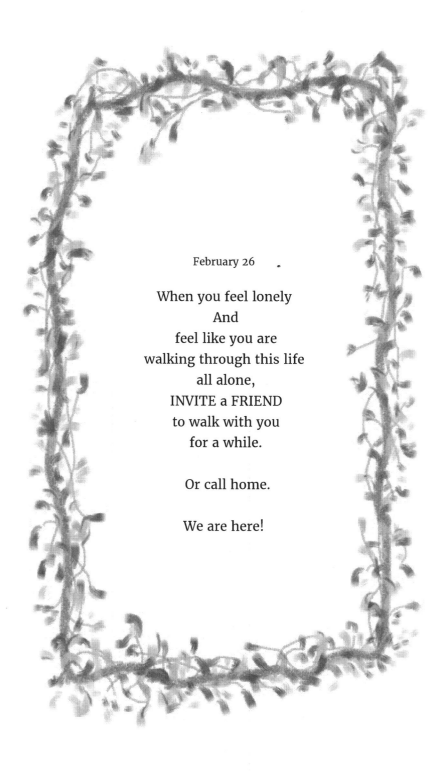

February 26

When you feel lonely
And
feel like you are
walking through this life
all alone,
INVITE a FRIEND
to walk with you
for a while.

Or call home.

We are here!

February 27

It's okay
to feel sad,
or lonely,
or depressed,
or unmotivated.

Sometimes
we all need
a couch and blanket day.

Just
don't stay there
too long.

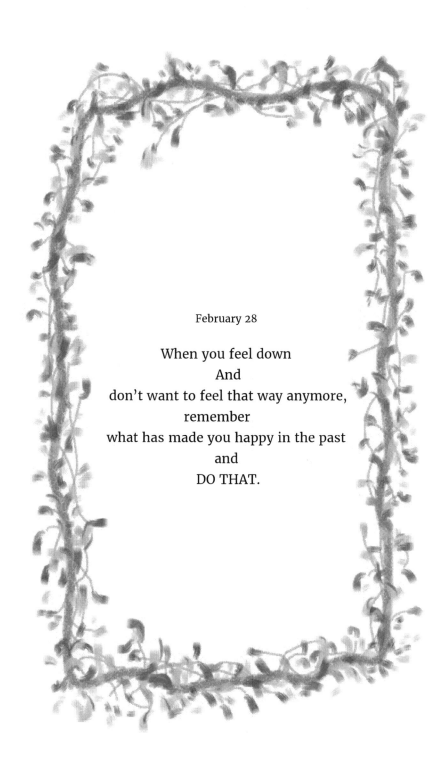

February 28

When you feel down
And
don't want to feel that way anymore,
remember
what has made you happy in the past
and
DO THAT.

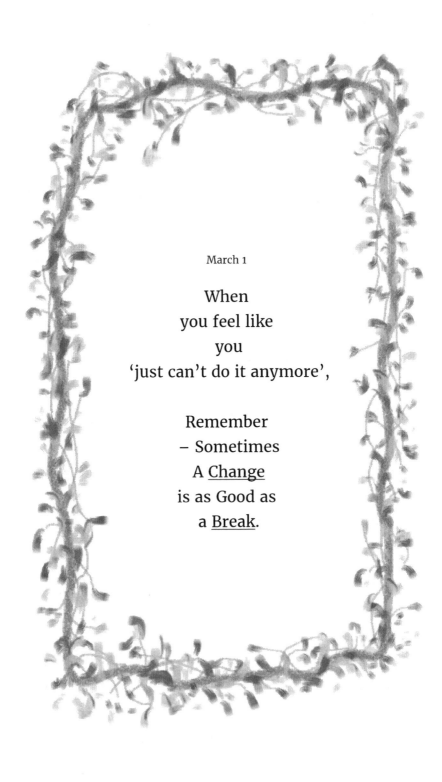

March 1

When
you feel like
you
'just can't do it anymore',

Remember
– Sometimes
A <u>Change</u>
is as Good as
a <u>Break</u>.

March 2

Marriages,
like friendships,
require maintenance.

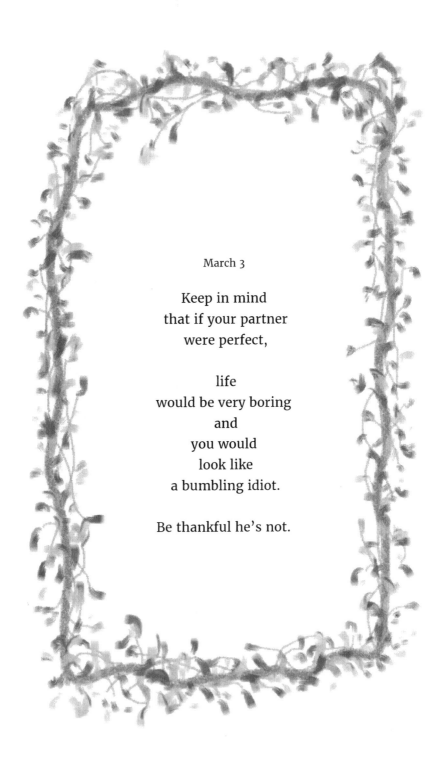

March 3

Keep in mind
that if your partner
were perfect,

life
would be very boring
and
you would
look like
a bumbling idiot.

Be thankful he's not.

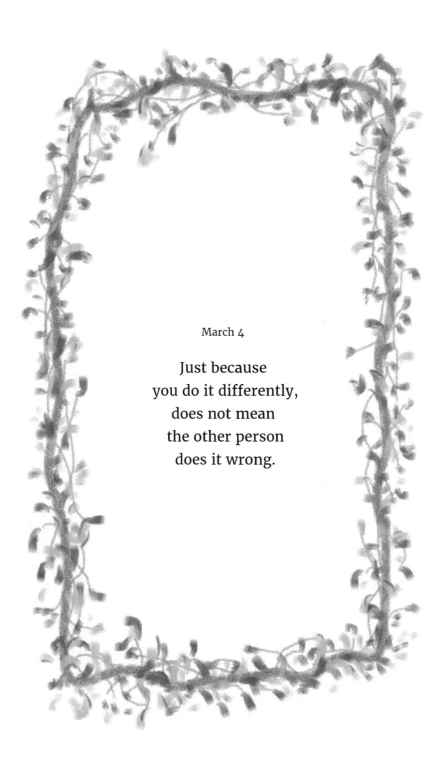

March 4

Just because
you do it differently,
does not mean
the other person
does it wrong.

March 5

NOBODY
HAS TO
stay in a marriage.

It's a
voluntary
arrangement.

March 6

When somebody
does something
to help you out,
it's best
not to criticize
the WAY
they do it.

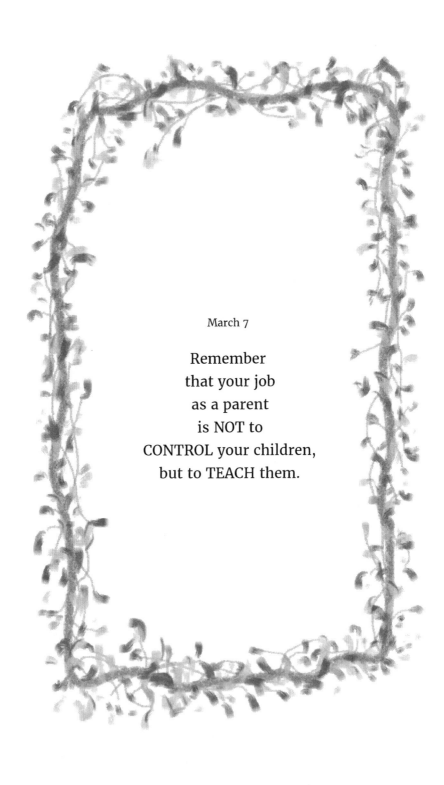

March 7

Remember
that your job
as a parent
is NOT to
CONTROL your children,
but to TEACH them.

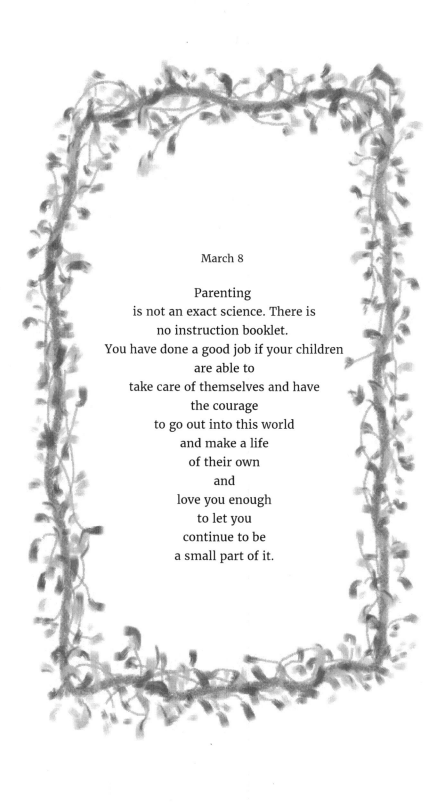

March 8

Parenting
is not an exact science. There is
no instruction booklet.
You have done a good job if your children
are able to
take care of themselves and have
the courage
to go out into this world
and make a life
of their own
and
love you enough
to let you
continue to be
a small part of it.

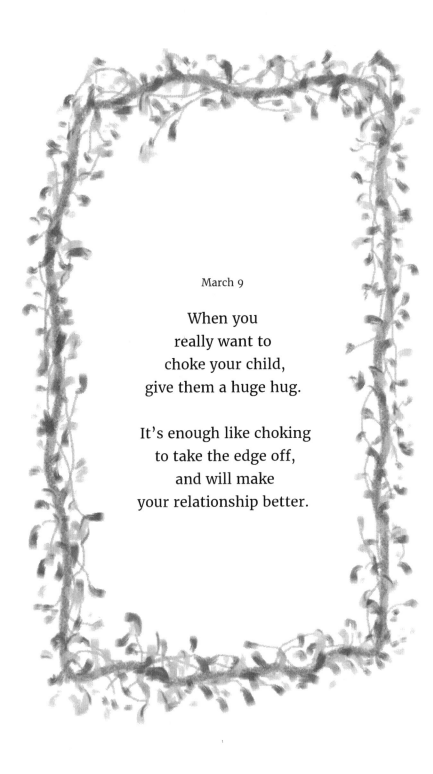

March 9

When you
really want to
choke your child,
give them a huge hug.

It's enough like choking
to take the edge off,
and will make
your relationship better.

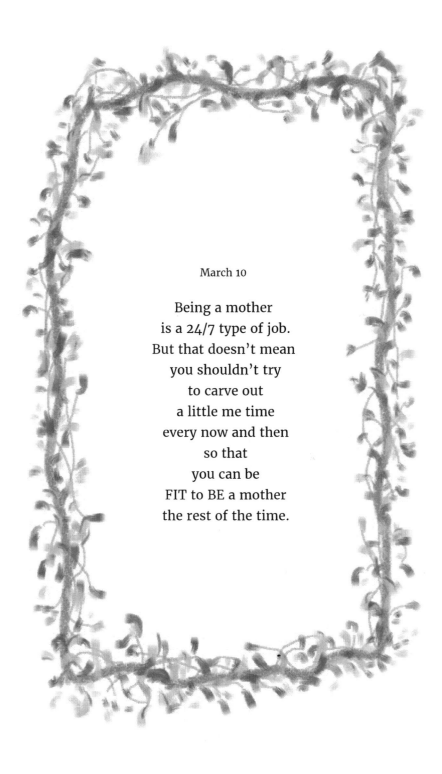

March 10

Being a mother
is a 24/7 type of job.
But that doesn't mean
you shouldn't try
to carve out
a little me time
every now and then
so that
you can be
FIT to BE a mother
the rest of the time.

March 11

Being
a full-time mom
is a temporary job,
you should have
something else
to fall back on
when it's over.

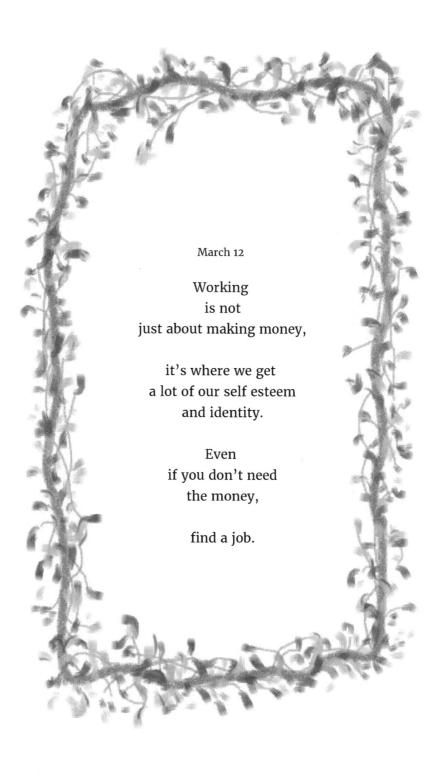

March 12

Working
is not
just about making money,

it's where we get
a lot of our self esteem
and identity.

Even
if you don't need
the money,

find a job.

March 13

**Learning
is a
lifetime event.**

Don't stop.

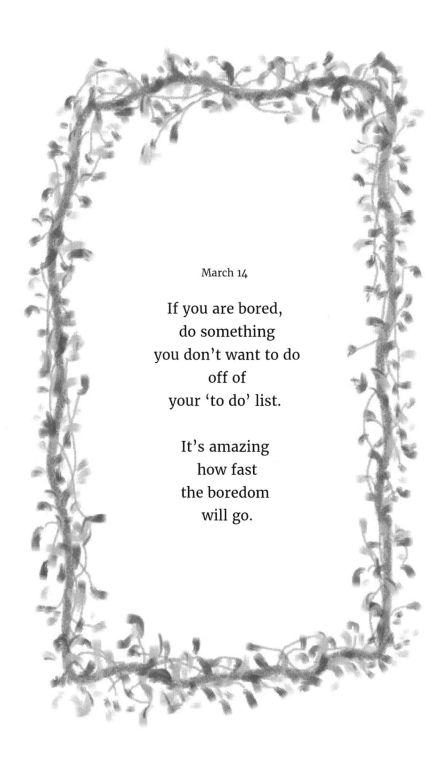

March 14

If you are bored,
do something
you don't want to do
off of
your 'to do' list.

It's amazing
how fast
the boredom
will go.

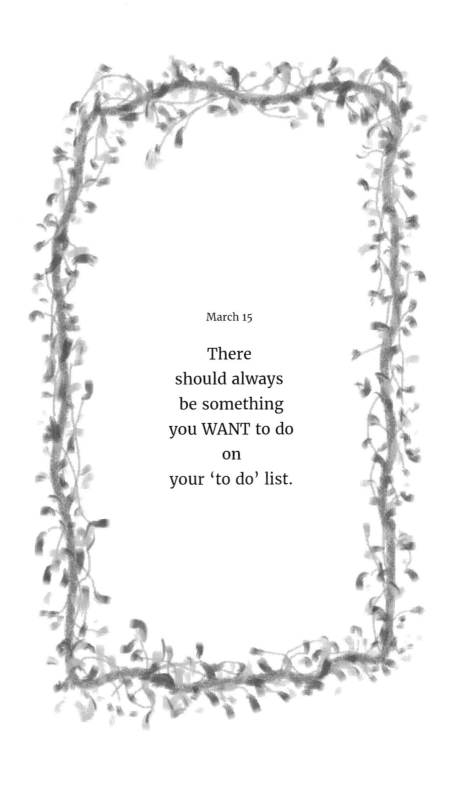

March 15

There
should always
be something
you WANT to do
on
your 'to do' list.

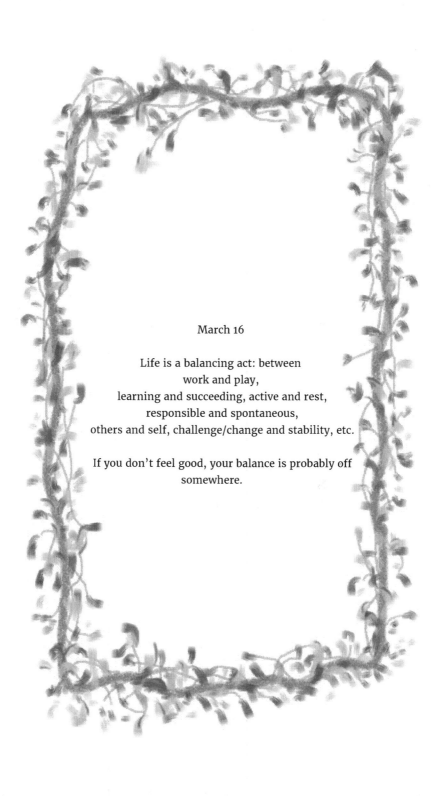

March 16

Life is a balancing act: between
work and play,
learning and succeeding, active and rest,
responsible and spontaneous,
others and self, challenge/change and stability, etc.

If you don't feel good, your balance is probably off
somewhere.

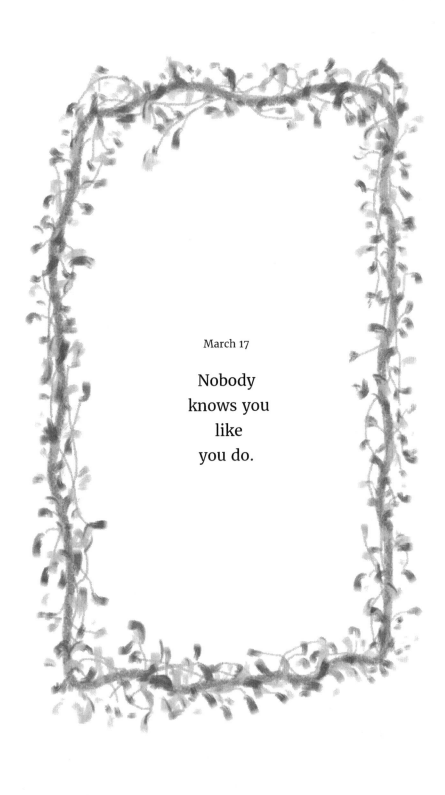

March 17

**Nobody
knows you
like
you do.**

March 18

You
are strong.

Be confident.

March 19

You might not
have all the answers,

but if
you've got the question,
it's a
good start.

March 20

Just because
someone drives you crazy, does not mean
you can't love them,
but
it might mean
you can't live with them.

March 21

If you
lay down like a rug
in front of someone
often enough,
eventually
they will walk on you.

It doesn't matter
HOW good a person
they are.

March 22

If
you don't tell
someone
what you want or need
in a relationship,
you
should not be
surprised
when you don't get it.

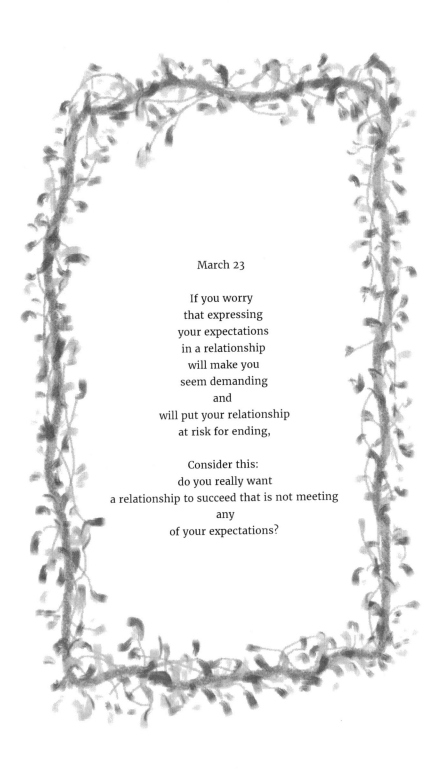

March 23

If you worry
that expressing
your expectations
in a relationship
will make you
seem demanding
and
will put your relationship
at risk for ending,

Consider this:
do you really want
a relationship to succeed that is not meeting
any
of your expectations?

March 24

If
you do not expect anything from
someone,
you are sending them
a message
that you don't think
they are capable
of
meeting expectations.

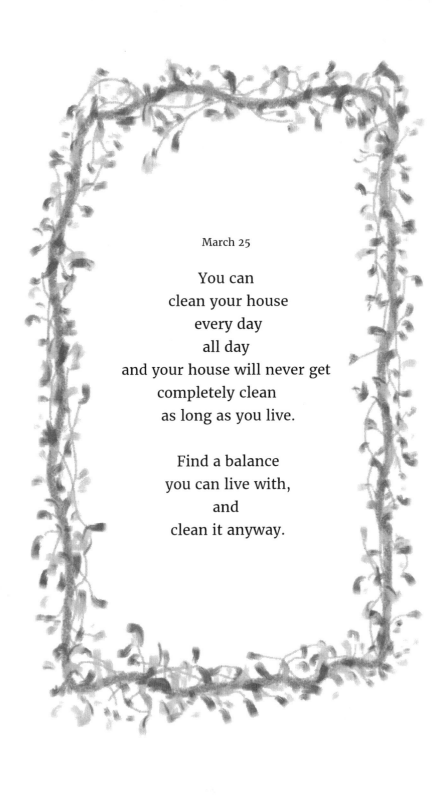

March 25

You can
clean your house
every day
all day
and your house will never get
completely clean
as long as you live.

Find a balance
you can live with,
and
clean it anyway.

March 26

Letting
someone you love
struggle
is a sign
that you believe in them.

They can do it
And
if they fail
in the attempt,
they can handle it.

It's nice
when someone
believes in you,
especially
when life is hard.

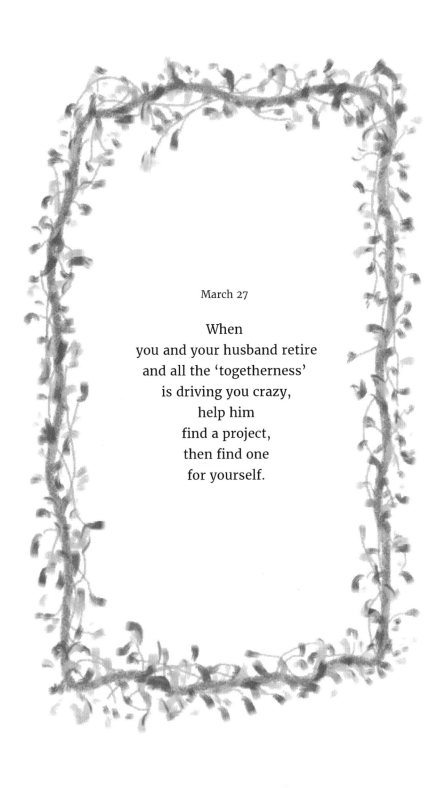

March 27

When
you and your husband retire
and all the 'togetherness'
is driving you crazy,
help him
find a project,
then find one
for yourself.

March 28

Remember
to make good memories
for you and your family.

It's hard work
And
takes a ton of time,

but it's worth it.

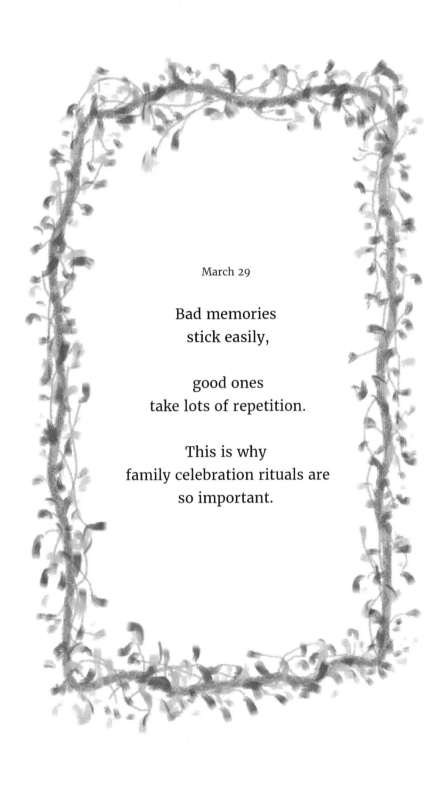

March 29

Bad memories
stick easily,

good ones
take lots of repetition.

This is why
family celebration rituals are
so important.

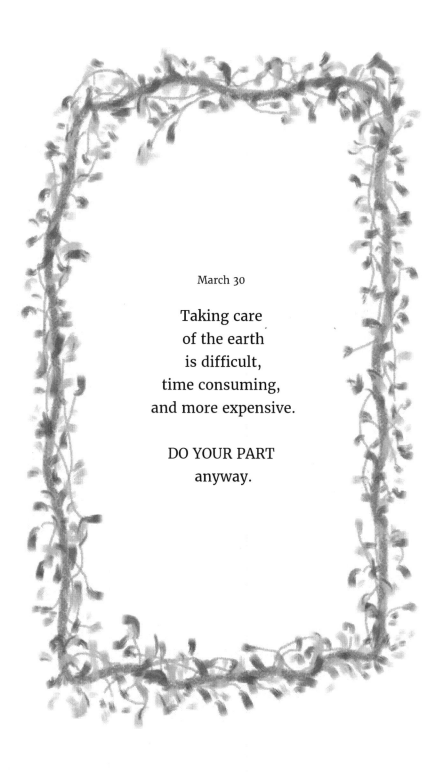

March 30

Taking care
of the earth
is difficult,
time consuming,
and more expensive.

DO YOUR PART
anyway.

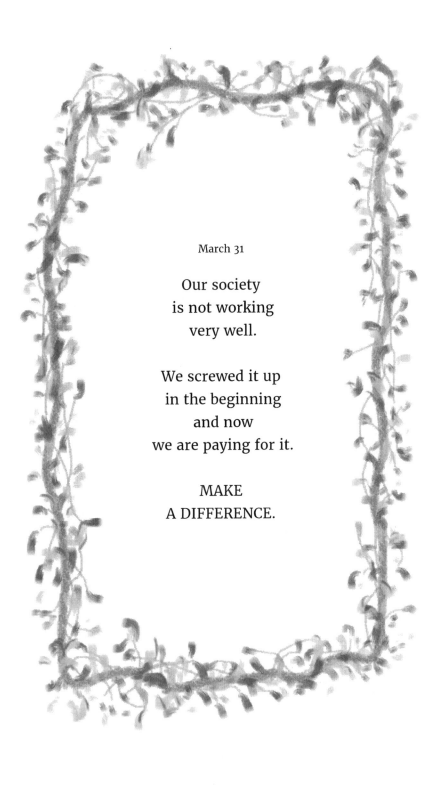

March 31

Our society
is not working
very well.

We screwed it up
in the beginning
and now
we are paying for it.

MAKE
A DIFFERENCE.

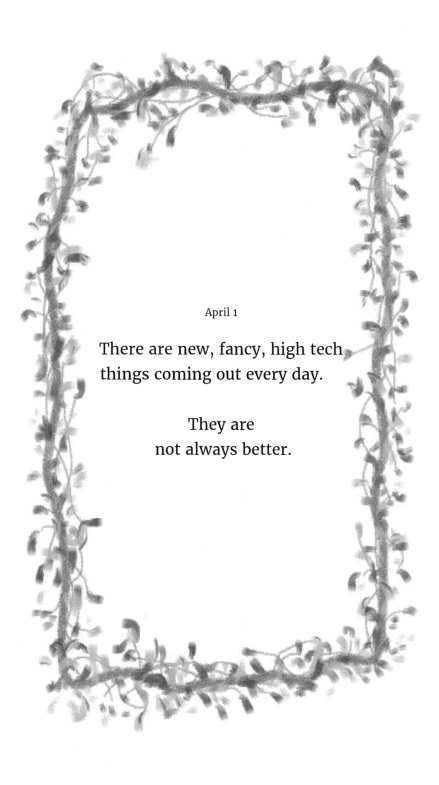

April 1

There are new, fancy, high tech
things coming out every day.

They are
not always better.

April 2

Look to the past
for some answers
to
today's
problems.

April 3

Staying super busy
all the time
can be
a way of avoiding problems.

Avoided problems
have a way
of surfacing
all at once
at the worst times,...

April 4

Exercise
is important

throughout
your life.

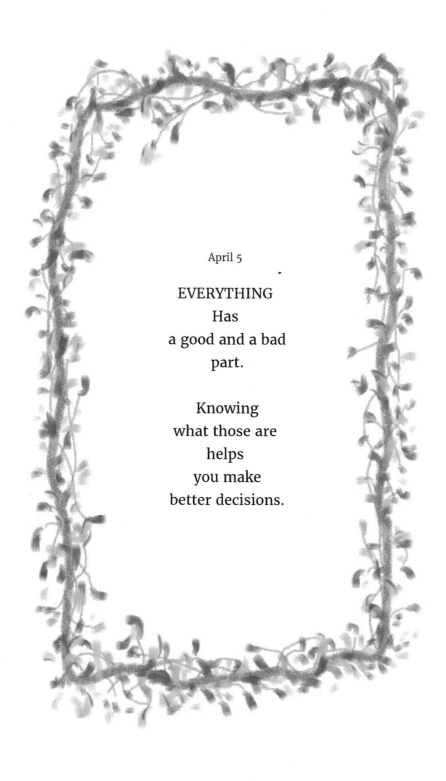

April 5

EVERYTHING
Has
a good and a bad
part.

Knowing
what those are
helps
you make
better decisions.

April 6

**Everything
is a choice
in
some way.**

April 7

Finding someone
that understands
and accepts you
while
still challenging you
to do your best
is
a real find.

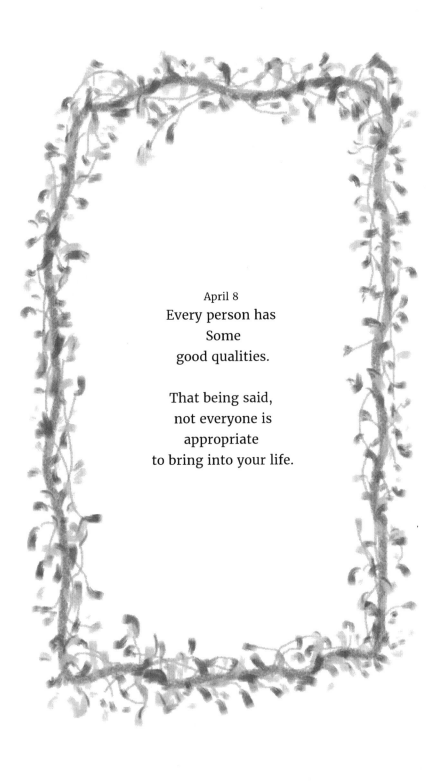

April 8
Every person has
Some
good qualities.

That being said,
not everyone is
appropriate
to bring into your life.

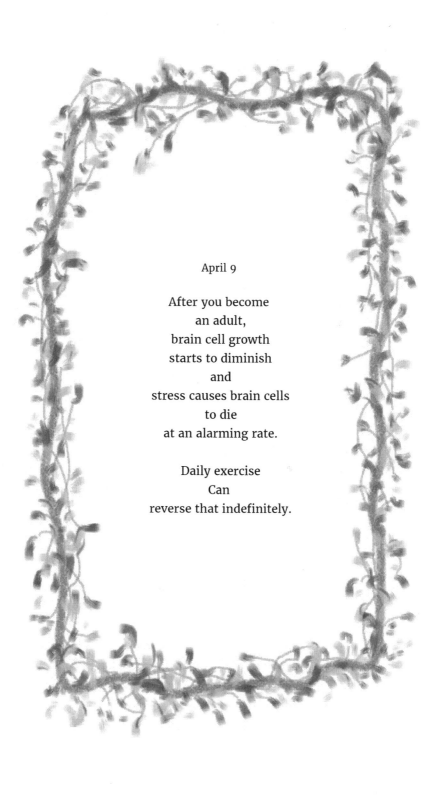

April 9

After you become
an adult,
brain cell growth
starts to diminish
and
stress causes brain cells
to die
at an alarming rate.

Daily exercise
Can
reverse that indefinitely.

April 10

As your life
gets more and more full,
it becomes
more and more difficult
to remain connected
with the ones that you love.

It seems
we take for granted
that the ones that we love will still be there
when we finally find time
to reconnect.
This is not the best idea, because sometimes
they are not
and we regret that.

Find time to connect
on a regular basis
with your loved ones.

It's important.

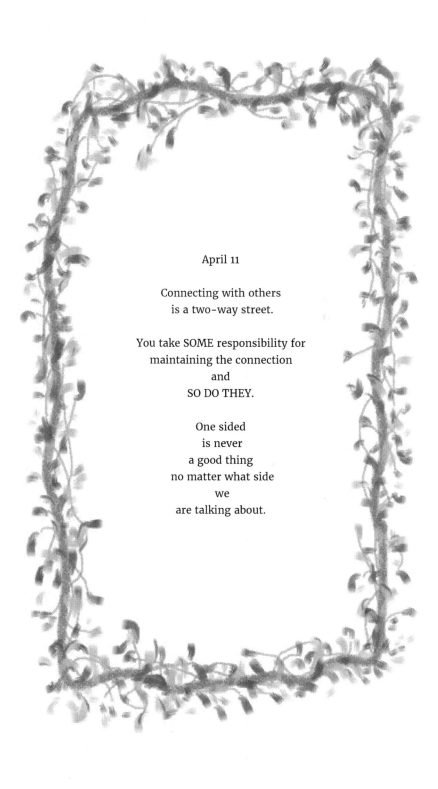

April 11

Connecting with others
is a two-way street.

You take SOME responsibility for
maintaining the connection
and
SO DO THEY.

One sided
is never
a good thing
no matter what side
we
are talking about.

April 12

Family
is about picking up someone's slack
periodically
when they have
over stretched themselves.

It's a way to allow
for more growth
for each individual
if everyone takes turns.

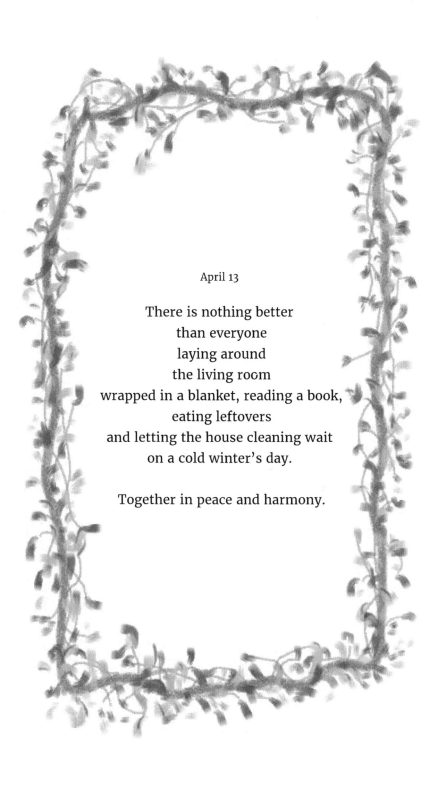

April 13

There is nothing better
than everyone
laying around
the living room
wrapped in a blanket, reading a book,
eating leftovers
and letting the house cleaning wait
on a cold winter's day.

Together in peace and harmony.

April 14

When your kids are small and
running around your ankles yelling
"Mommy, mommy" and
"I want"
and
you just want
it all to go away,...
stop,
take a breath
and know
that eventually
it WILL all go away,
and
you are gonna miss it.

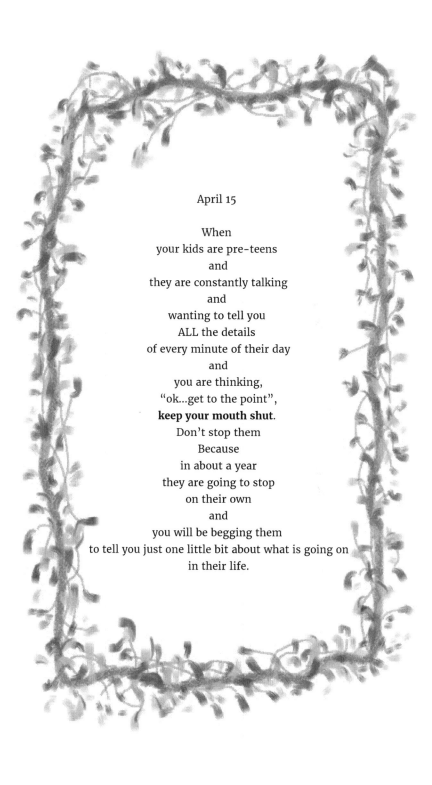

April 15

When
your kids are pre-teens
and
they are constantly talking
and
wanting to tell you
ALL the details
of every minute of their day
and
you are thinking,
"ok...get to the point",
keep your mouth shut.
Don't stop them
Because
in about a year
they are going to stop
on their own
and
you will be begging them
to tell you just one little bit about what is going on
in their life.

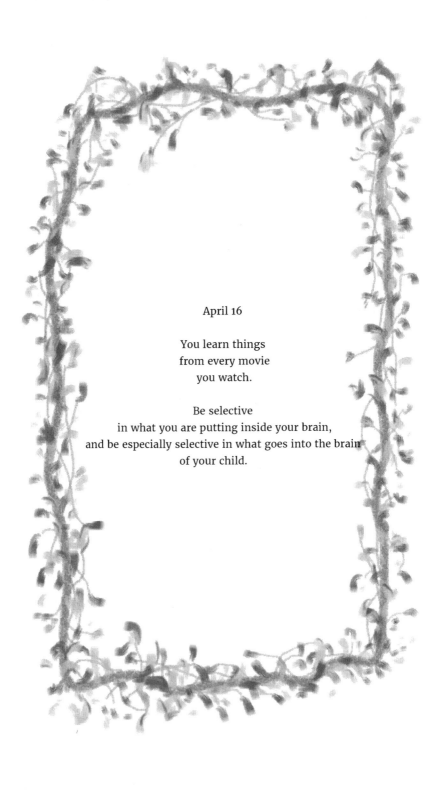

April 16

You learn things
from every movie
you watch.

Be selective
in what you are putting inside your brain,
and be especially selective in what goes into the brain
of your child.

April 17

You will have
LOTS
Of
responsibilities
throughout your life.

One of them
will always be
taking care of YOU.

April 18

Pets give you love
and
also tie you down.

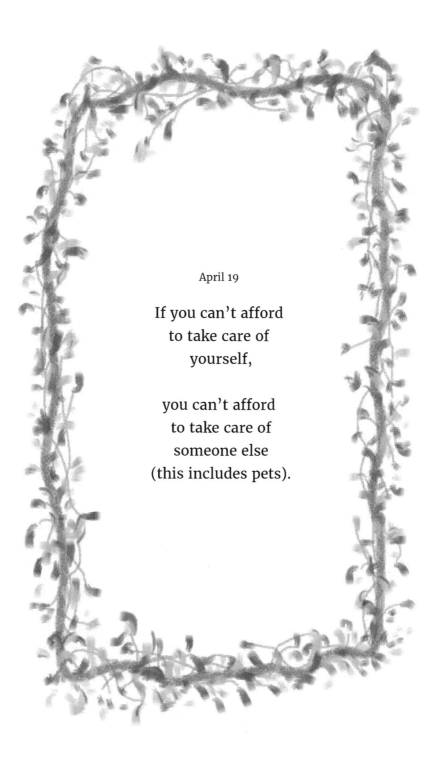

April 19

If you can't afford
to take care of
yourself,

you can't afford
to take care of
someone else
(this includes pets).

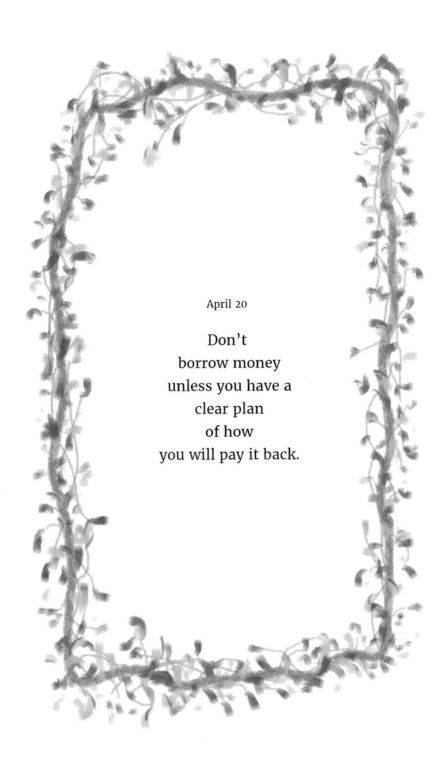

April 20

Don't
borrow money
unless you have a
clear plan
of how
you will pay it back.

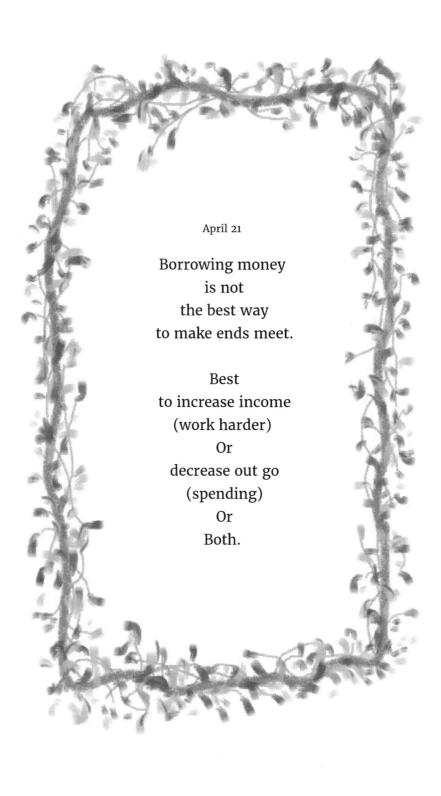

April 21

Borrowing money
is not
the best way
to make ends meet.

Best
to increase income
(work harder)
Or
decrease out go
(spending)
Or
Both.

April 22

Make a practice
of living
well below
your means (spending far less
than you make)
because
life
has a way
of surprising us
with emergency expenses.

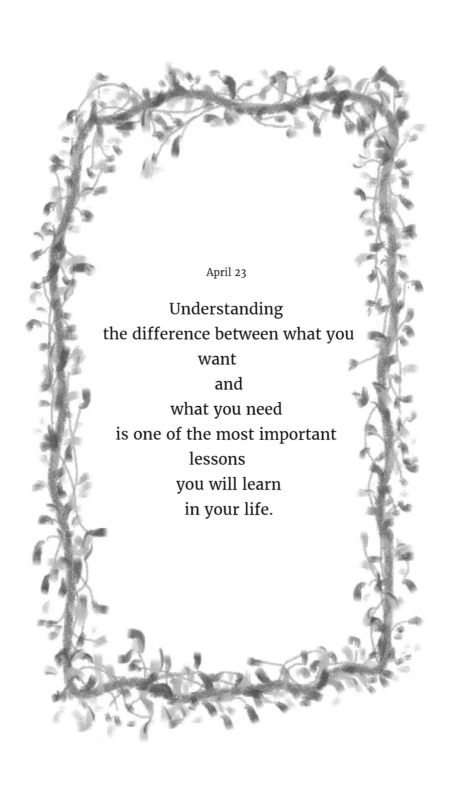

April 23

Understanding
the difference between what you
want
and
what you need
is one of the most important
lessons
you will learn
in your life.

April 24

Life
is not fair...

Thank GOD!

April 25

YOU
CAN DO IT!

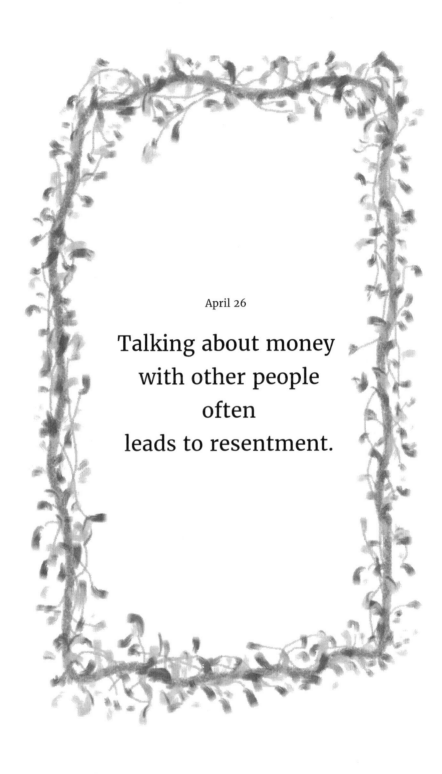

April 26

Talking about money
with other people
often
leads to resentment.

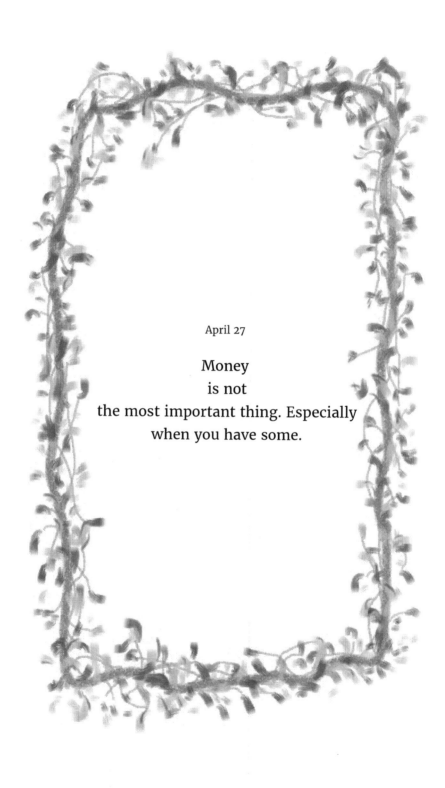

April 27

Money
is not
the most important thing. Especially
when you have some.

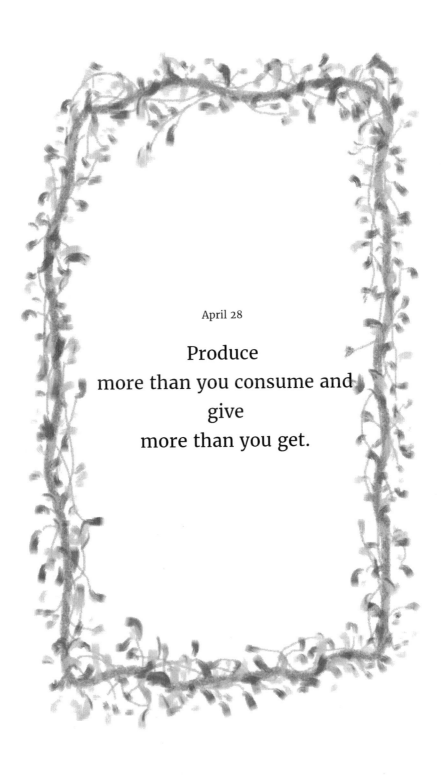

April 28

Produce
more than you consume and
give
more than you get.

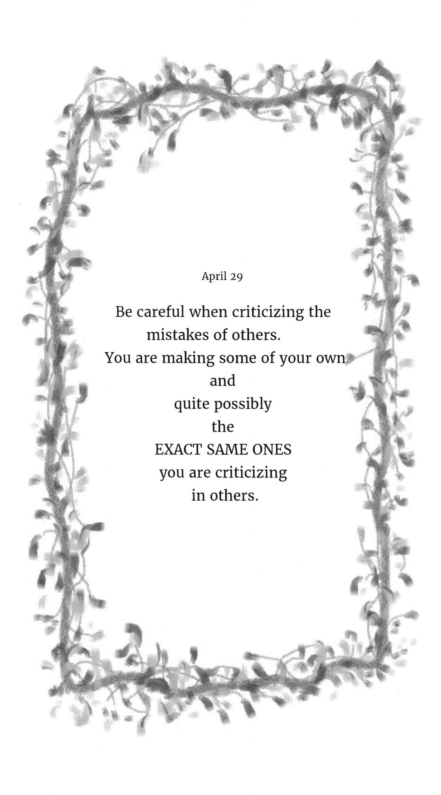

April 29

Be careful when criticizing the
mistakes of others.
You are making some of your own
and
quite possibly
the
EXACT SAME ONES
you are criticizing
in others.

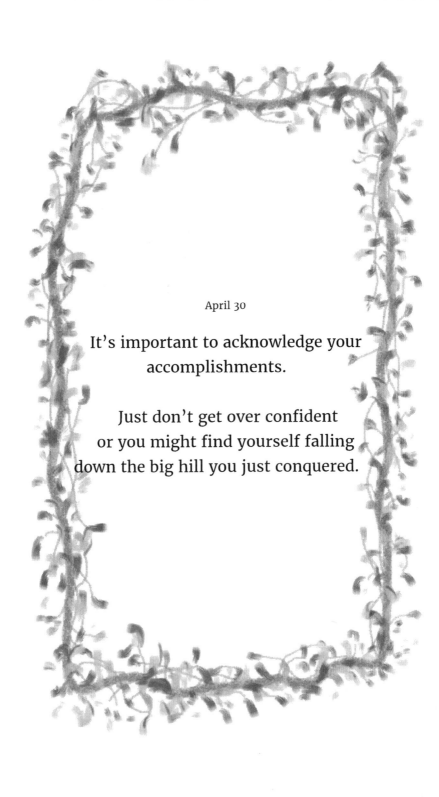

April 30

It's important to acknowledge your accomplishments.

Just don't get over confident
or you might find yourself falling
down the big hill you just conquered.

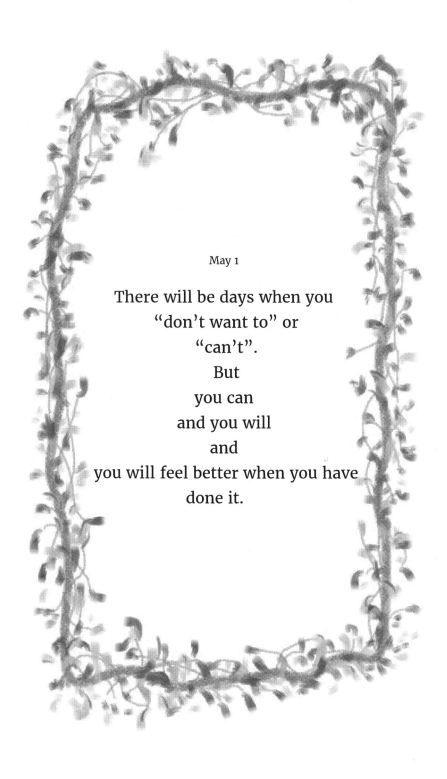

May 1

There will be days when you
"don't want to" or
"can't".
But
you can
and you will
and
you will feel better when you have
done it.

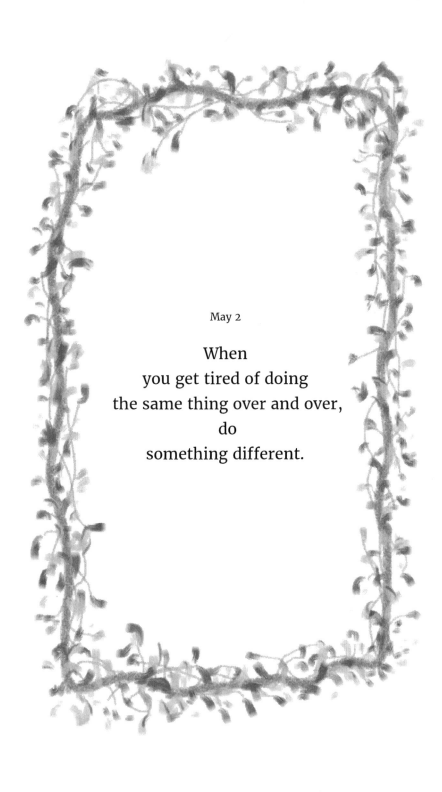

May 2

When
you get tired of doing
the same thing over and over,
do
something different.

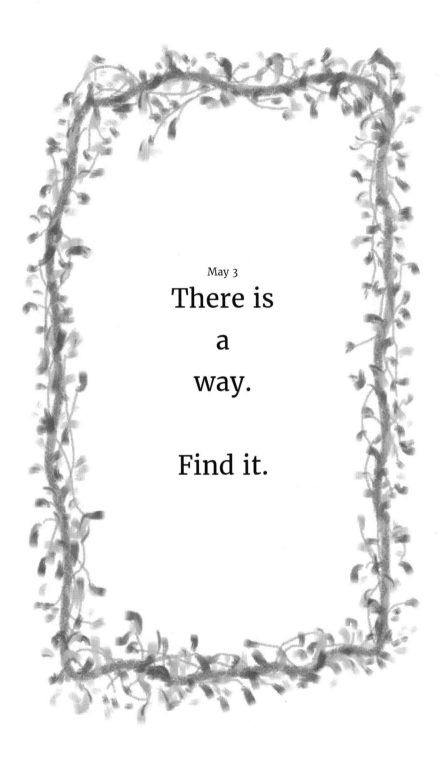

May 3

There is

a

way.

Find it.

May 4

It's easier
to do things
that you enjoy. So
find a way
to like
the hard things.

May 5

People
tell you
things
for
a reason.

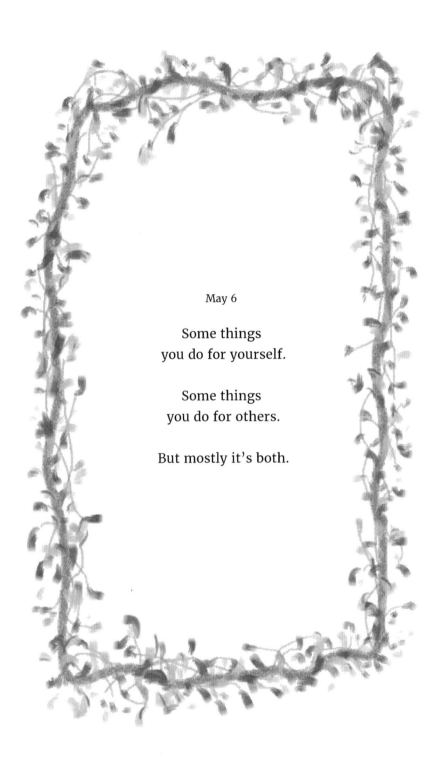

May 6

Some things
you do for yourself.

Some things
you do for others.

But mostly it's both.

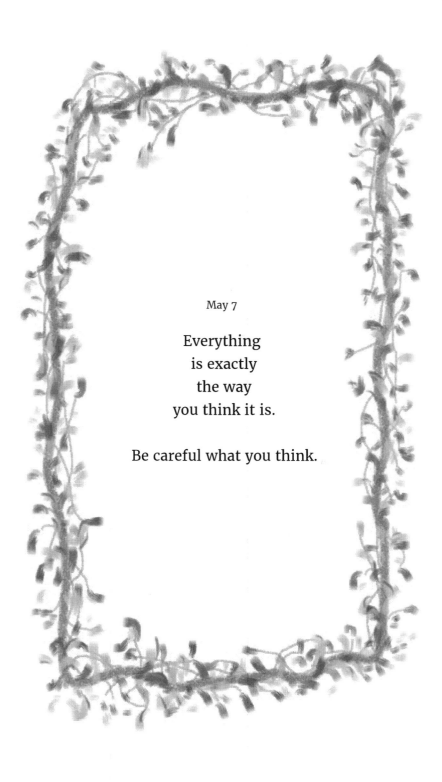

May 7

Everything
is exactly
the way
you think it is.

Be careful what you think.

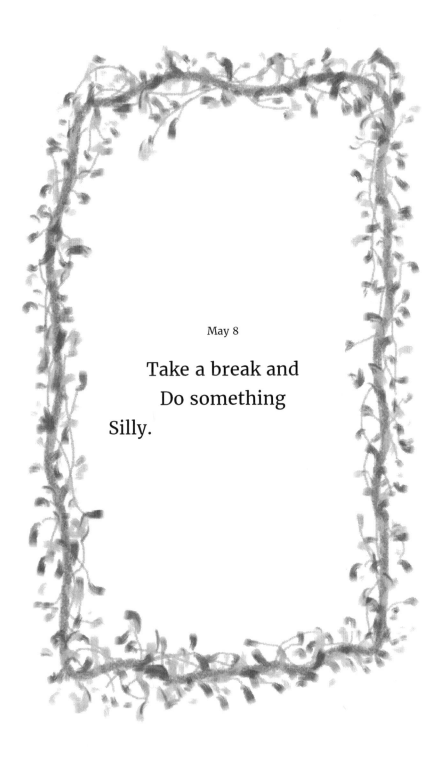

May 8

Take a break and
Do something
Silly.

May 9

Being happy
is very hard
when
your attention
is focused
on the bad.

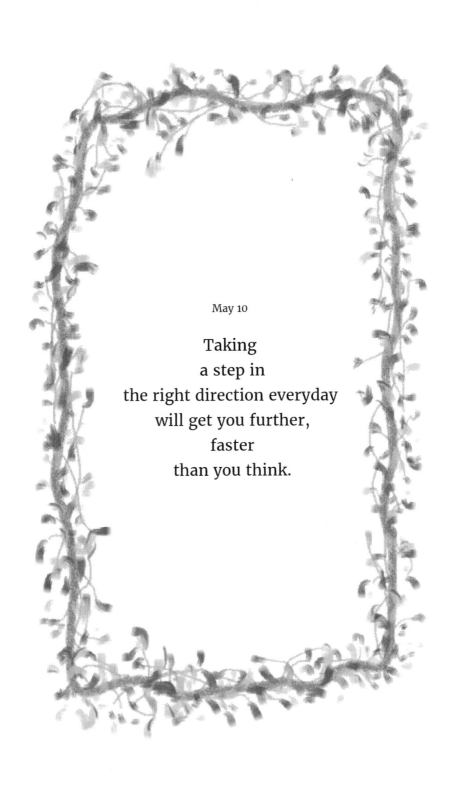

May 10

Taking
a step in
the right direction everyday
will get you further,
faster
than you think.

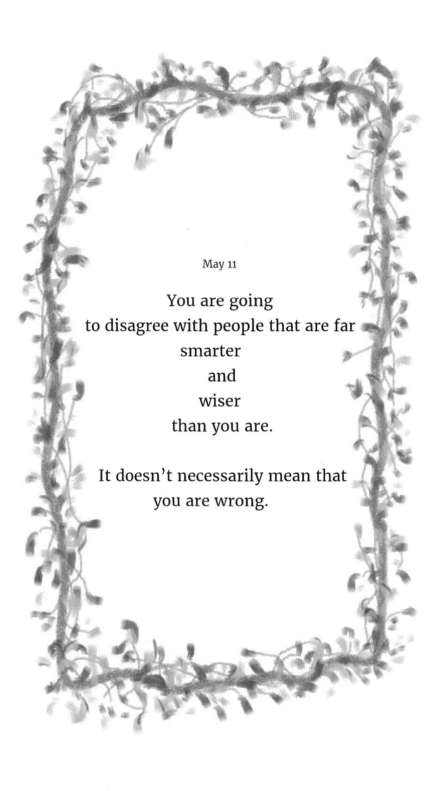

May 11

You are going
to disagree with people that are far
smarter
and
wiser
than you are.

It doesn't necessarily mean that
you are wrong.

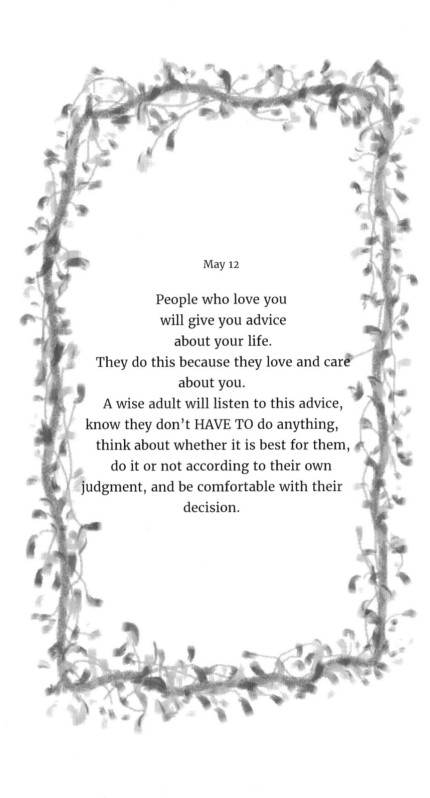

May 12

People who love you
will give you advice
about your life.
They do this because they love and care
about you.
A wise adult will listen to this advice,
know they don't HAVE TO do anything,
think about whether it is best for them,
do it or not according to their own
judgment, and be comfortable with their
decision.

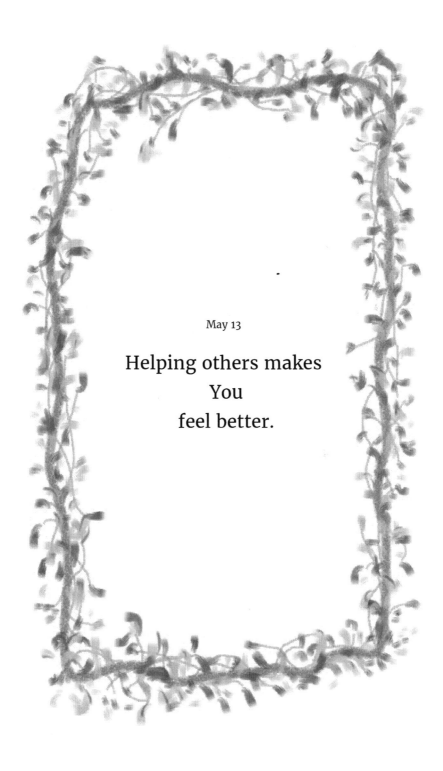

May 13

Helping others makes
You
feel better.

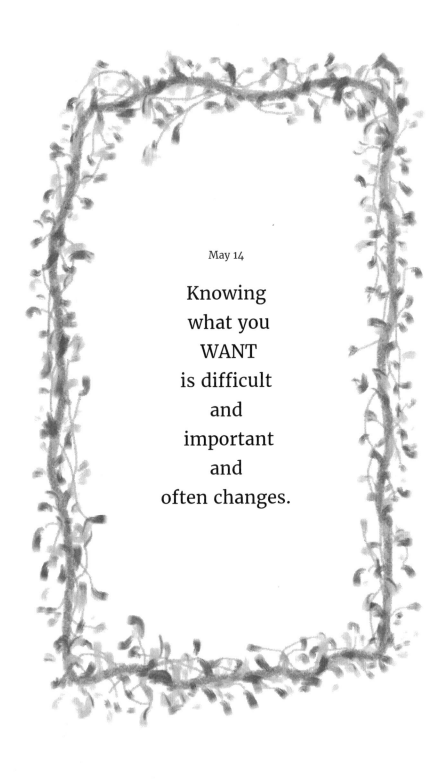

May 14

Knowing
what you
WANT
is difficult
and
important
and
often changes.

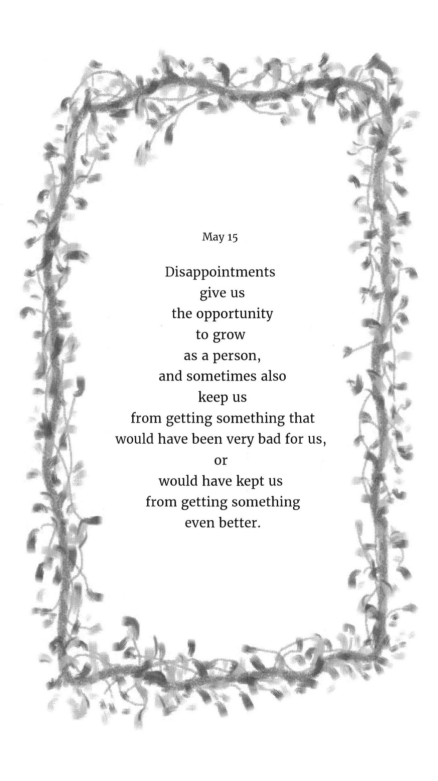

May 15

Disappointments
give us
the opportunity
to grow
as a person,
and sometimes also
keep us
from getting something that
would have been very bad for us,
or
would have kept us
from getting something
even better.

May 16

Sometimes
it feels like
our entire plan for life
just got taken away from us.

It was the wrong plan.

A better plan will soon surface
if we look.

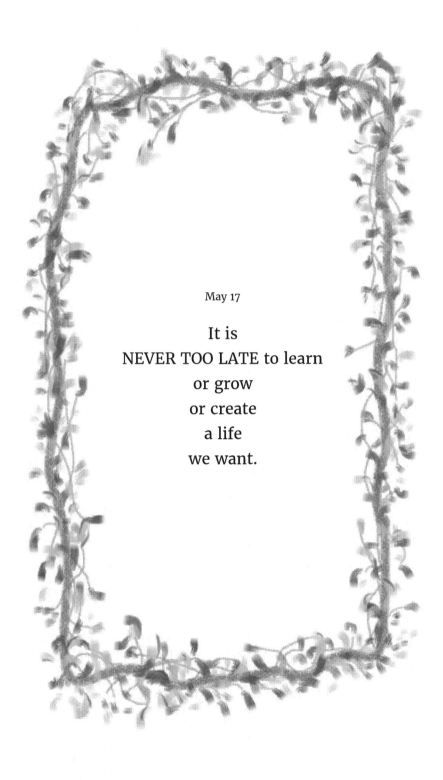

May 17

It is
NEVER TOO LATE to learn
or grow
or create
a life
we want.

May 18

Being
difficult
isn't
a bad thing.

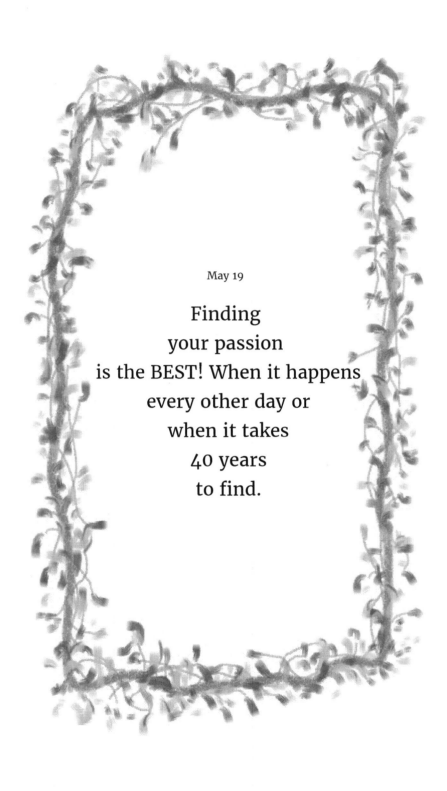

May 19

Finding
your passion
is the BEST! When it happens
every other day or
when it takes
40 years
to find.

May 20

You shouldn't tell just anyone EVERYTHING about your life.

That includes posting on social media.

May 21

Everyone needs a kick in the butt
sometimes.

Find a person who is willing to do
that for you and
go to them
when needed.

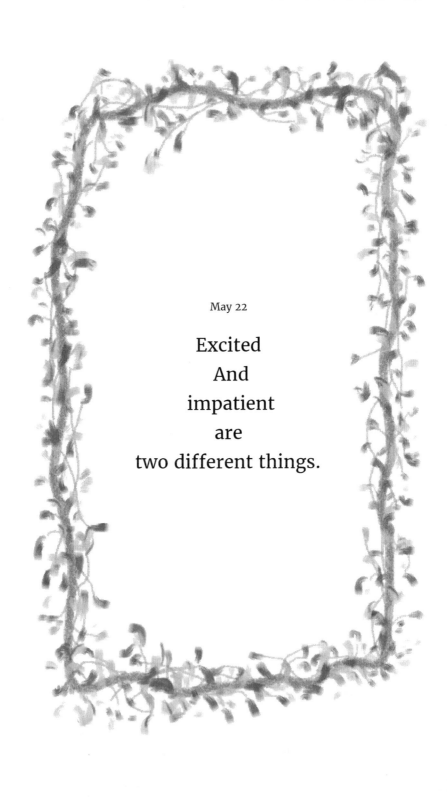

May 22

Excited
And
impatient
are
two different things.

May 23

Excited
And
scared
are the same emotions with a
different label – one positive,
one negative.

Decide how you want to label
things.

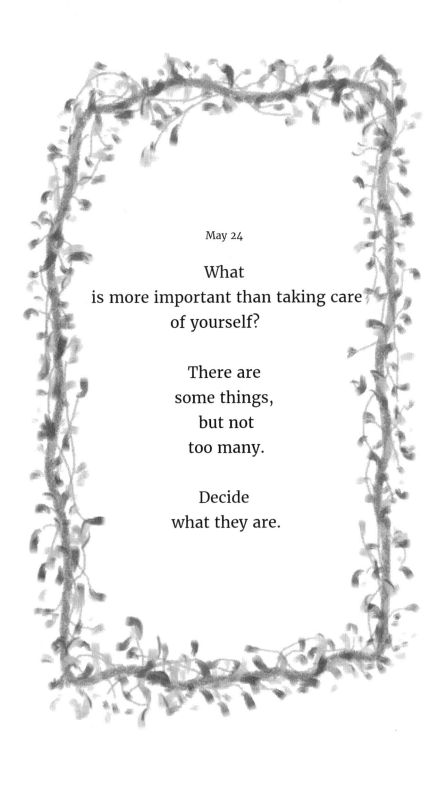

May 24

What
is more important than taking care
of yourself?

There are
some things,
but not
too many.

Decide
what they are.

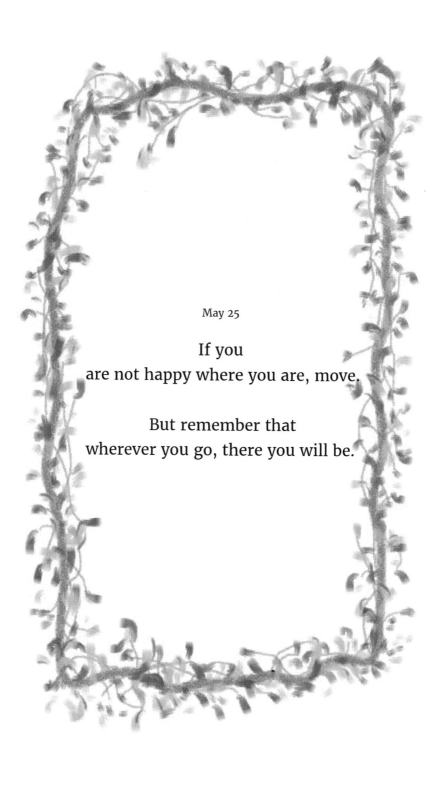

May 25

If you
are not happy where you are, move.

But remember that
wherever you go, there you will be.

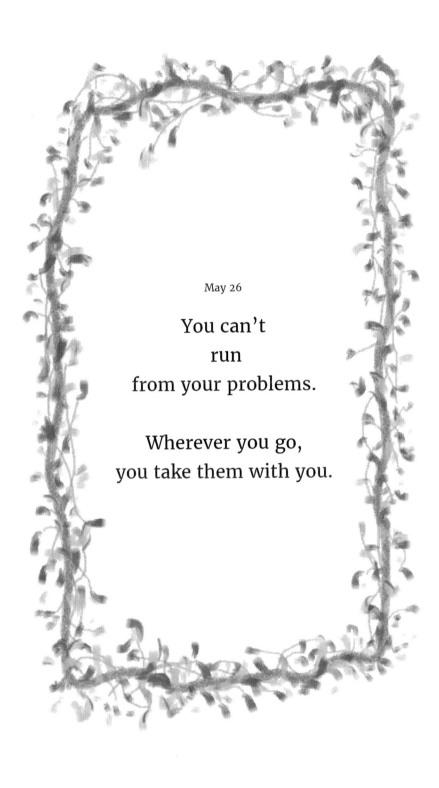

May 26

You can't
run
from your problems.

Wherever you go,
you take them with you.

May 27

Parenting
is a job
that never ends, and
changes constantly.

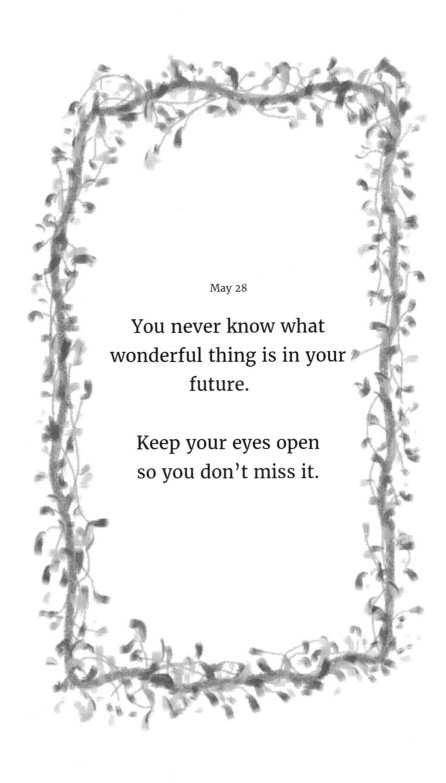

May 28

You never know what
wonderful thing is in your
future.

Keep your eyes open
so you don't miss it.

May 29

Letting
your children grow up
is difficult.

But
what happens if you don't.

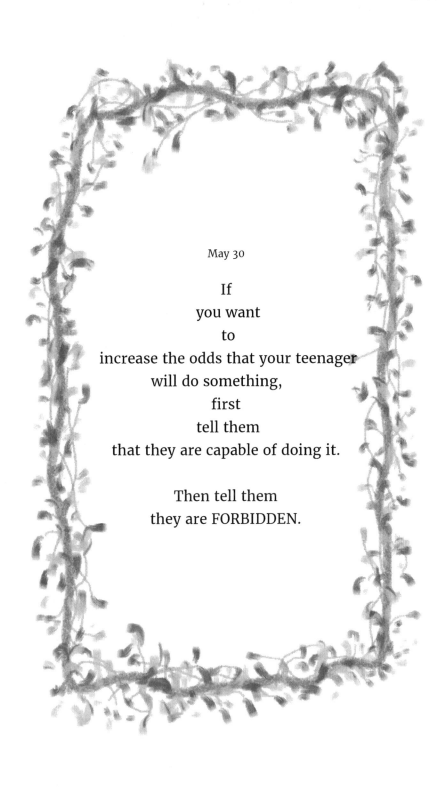

May 30

If
you want
to
increase the odds that your teenager
will do something,
first
tell them
that they are capable of doing it.

Then tell them
they are FORBIDDEN.

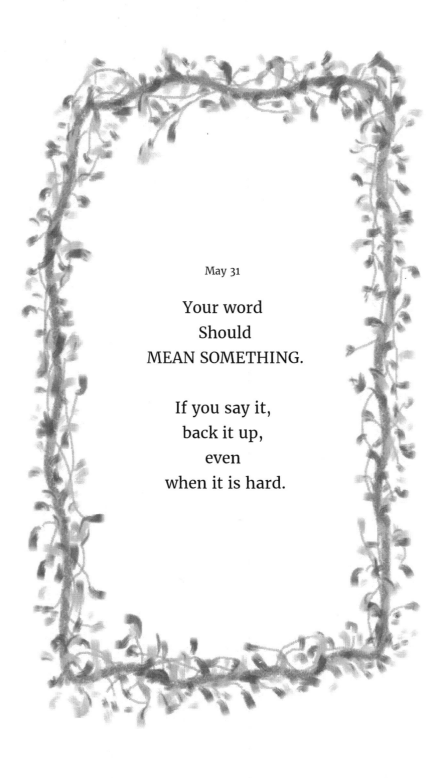

May 31

Your word
Should
MEAN SOMETHING.

If you say it,
back it up,
even
when it is hard.

June 1

Don't say
things
that you
don't mean,

especially
to your children.

June 2

FINISHING
what you start
is a
BIG DEAL!

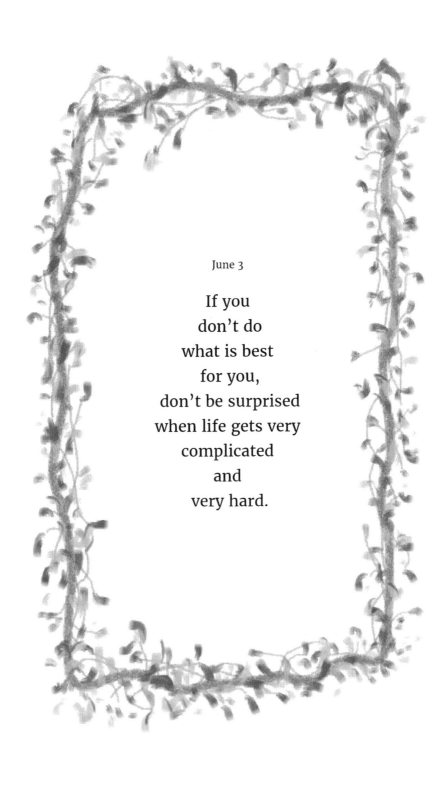

June 3

If you
don't do
what is best
for you,
don't be surprised
when life gets very
complicated
and
very hard.

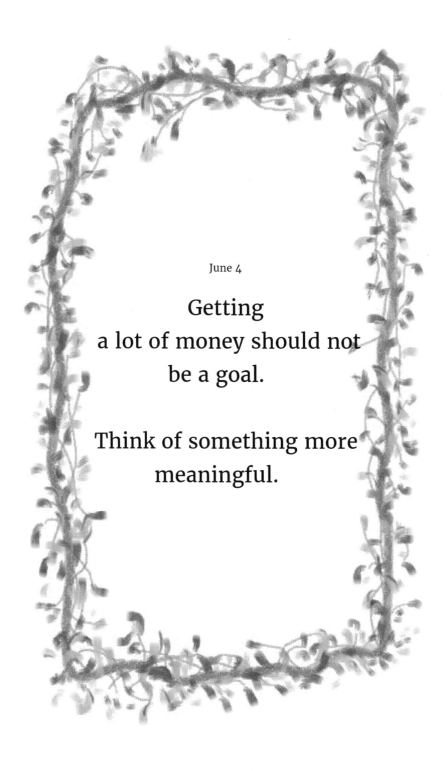

June 4

Getting
a lot of money should not
be a goal.

Think of something more
meaningful.

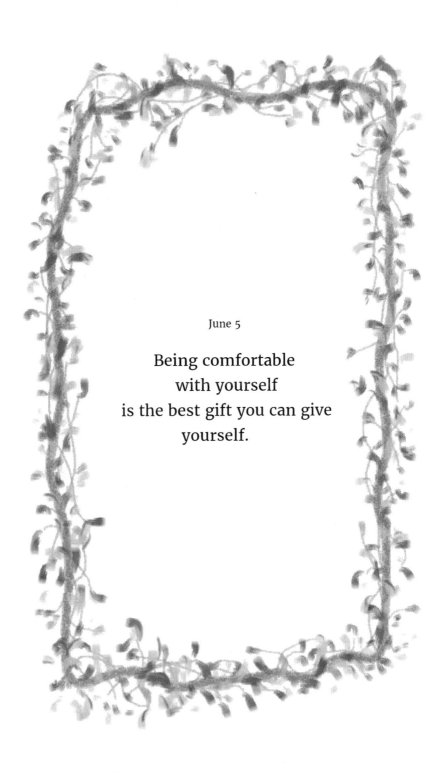

June 5

Being comfortable
with yourself
is the best gift you can give
yourself.

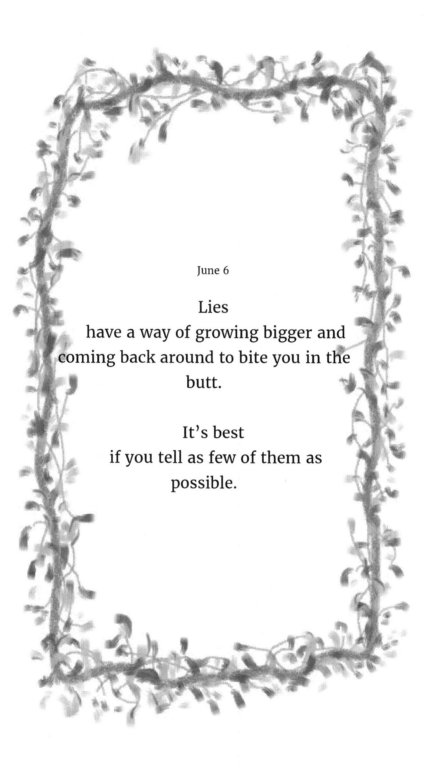

June 6

Lies
have a way of growing bigger and
coming back around to bite you in the
butt.

It's best
if you tell as few of them as
possible.

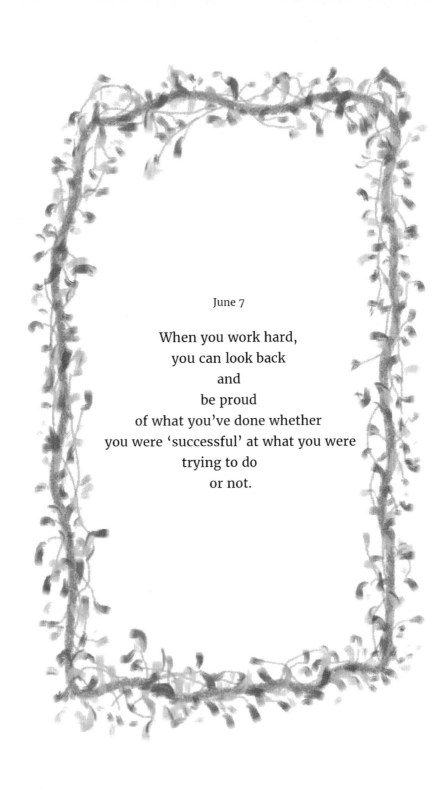

June 7

When you work hard,
you can look back
and
be proud
of what you've done whether
you were 'successful' at what you were
trying to do
or not.

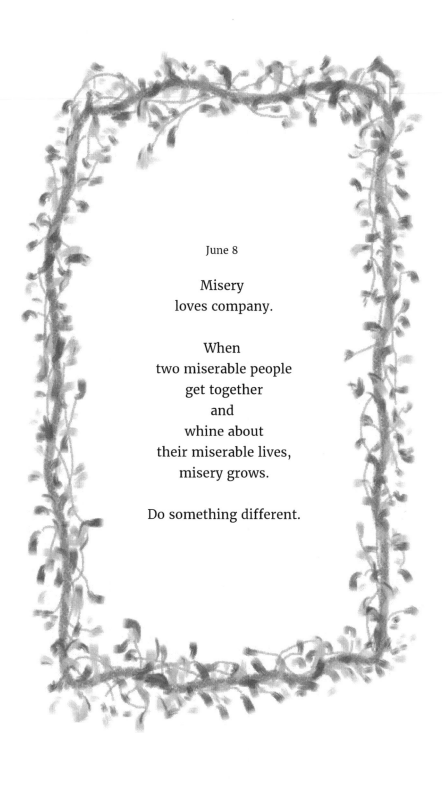

June 8

Misery
loves company.

When
two miserable people
get together
and
whine about
their miserable lives,
misery grows.

Do something different.

June 9

Who
you spend your time with
says a lot about who you are.

Choose
your friends wisely.

June 10

Life
will throw
many difficult things at you.
Don't give up.
The good
is just past the bad, but
you've got
to get to
the other side.

June 11

If you pay attention
to only the bad stuff, that is all you will
remember
and when you look back at your life
it will seem that you have had a bad life.
The same is true
for good.
Try to remember
the good
and carry the lessons from
the challenges.

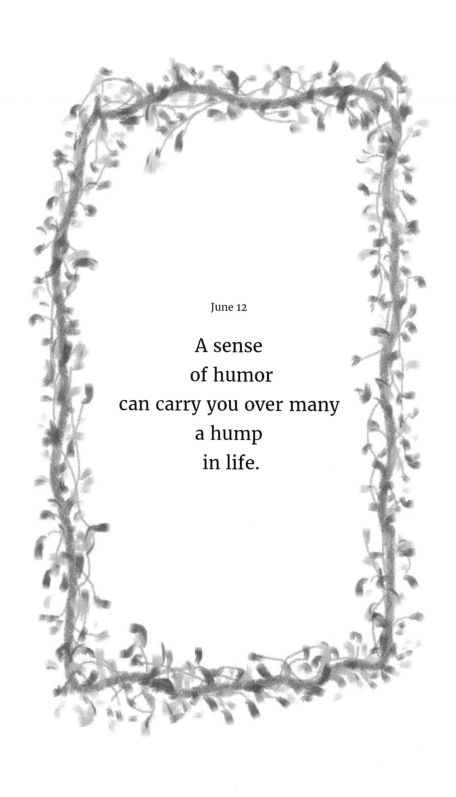

June 12

A sense
of humor
can carry you over many
a hump
in life.

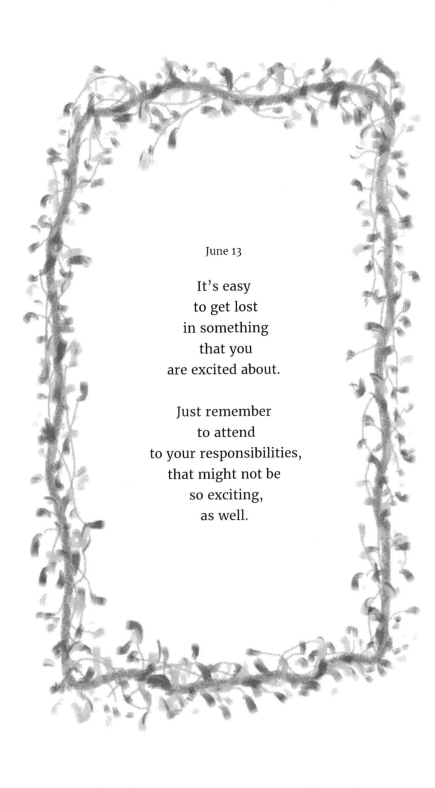

June 13

It's easy
to get lost
in something
that you
are excited about.

Just remember
to attend
to your responsibilities,
that might not be
so exciting,
as well.

June 14

It is
VERY difficult
to quit a habit.

Be careful
What
you make
a habit of.

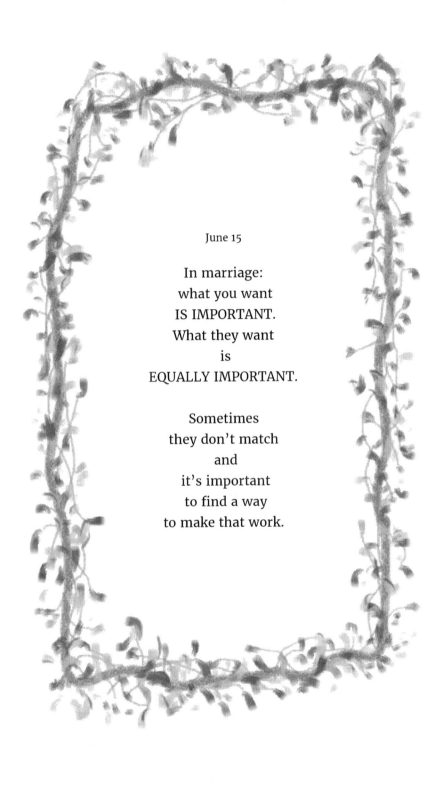

June 15

In marriage:
what you want
IS IMPORTANT.
What they want
is
EQUALLY IMPORTANT.

Sometimes
they don't match
and
it's important
to find a way
to make that work.

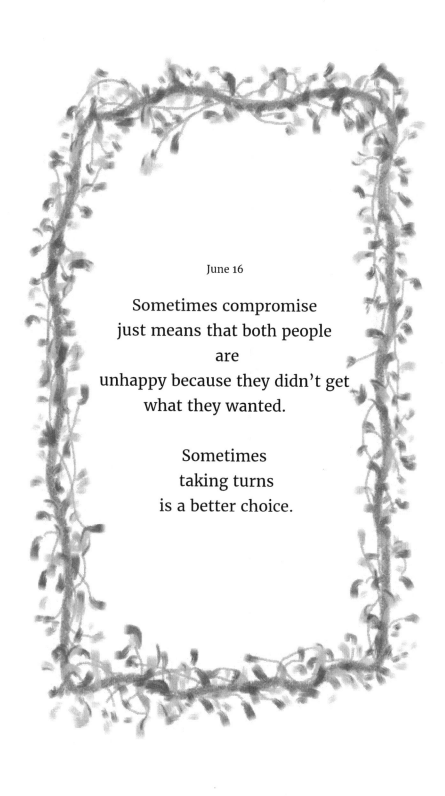

June 16

Sometimes compromise
just means that both people
are
unhappy because they didn't get
what they wanted.

Sometimes
taking turns
is a better choice.

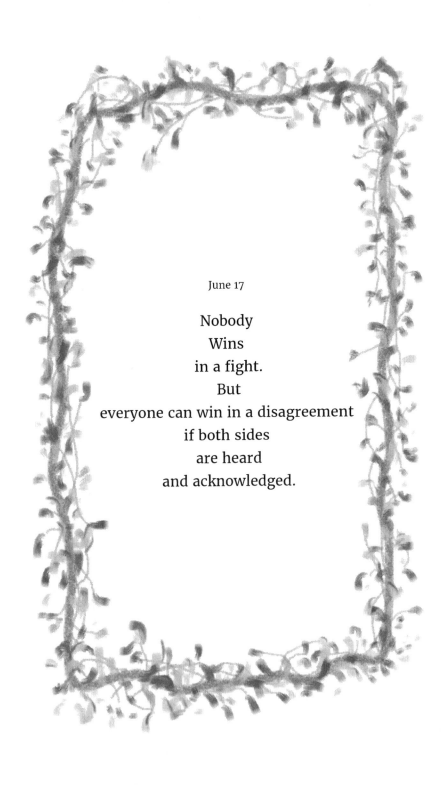

June 17

Nobody
Wins
in a fight.
But
everyone can win in a disagreement
if both sides
are heard
and acknowledged.

June 18

Never disagreeing
is NOT
A SOLUTION
in marriage..

It's a recipe
for
divorce.

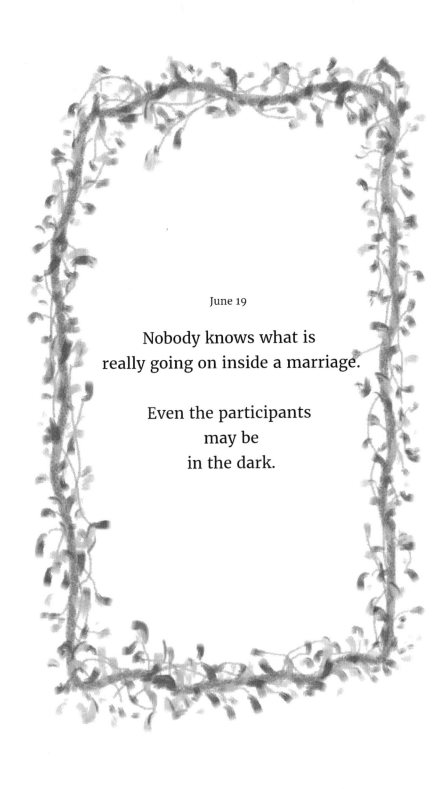

June 19

Nobody knows what is
really going on inside a marriage.

Even the participants
may be
in the dark.

June 20

Honest communication
is your
best shot
at a
good relationship of any kind.

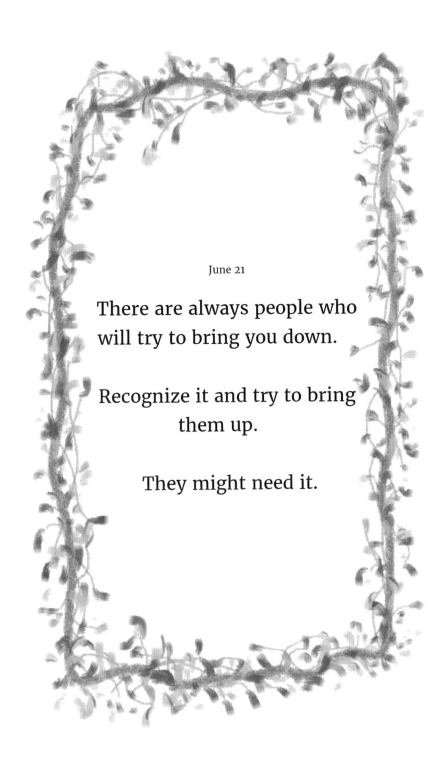

June 21

There are always people who
will try to bring you down.

Recognize it and try to bring
them up.

They might need it.

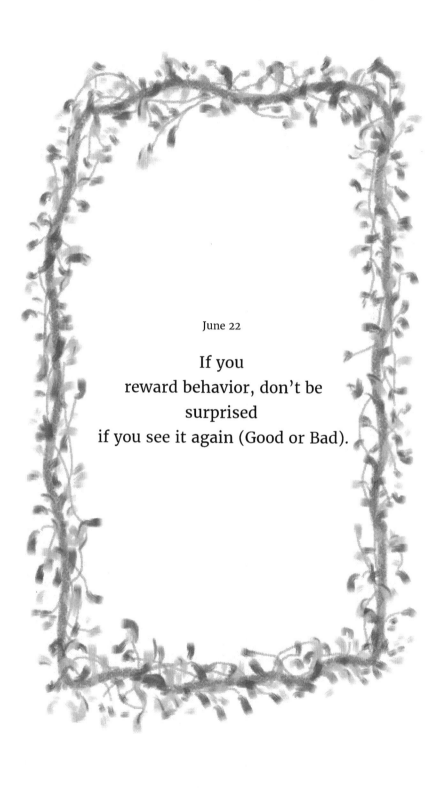

June 22

If you
reward behavior, don't be
surprised
if you see it again (Good or Bad).

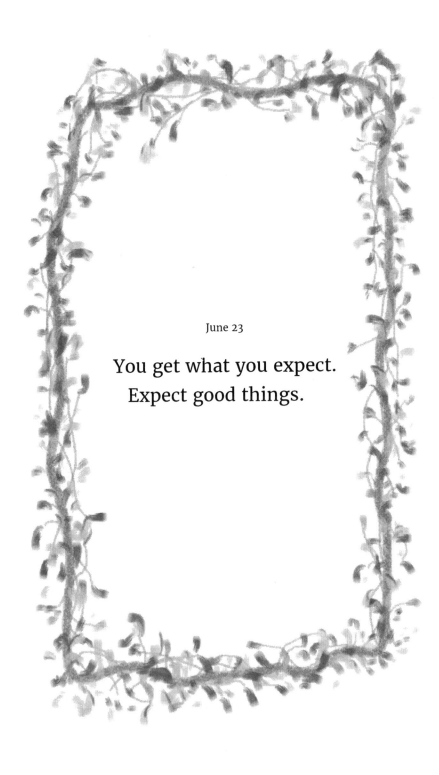

June 23

You get what you expect.
Expect good things.

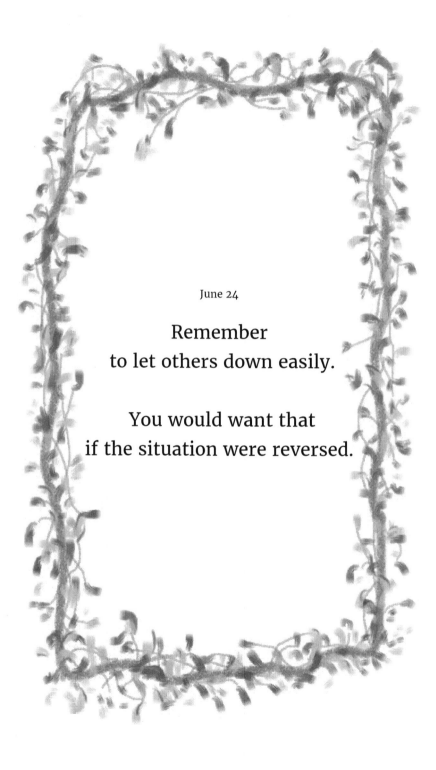

June 24

Remember
to let others down easily.

You would want that
if the situation were reversed.

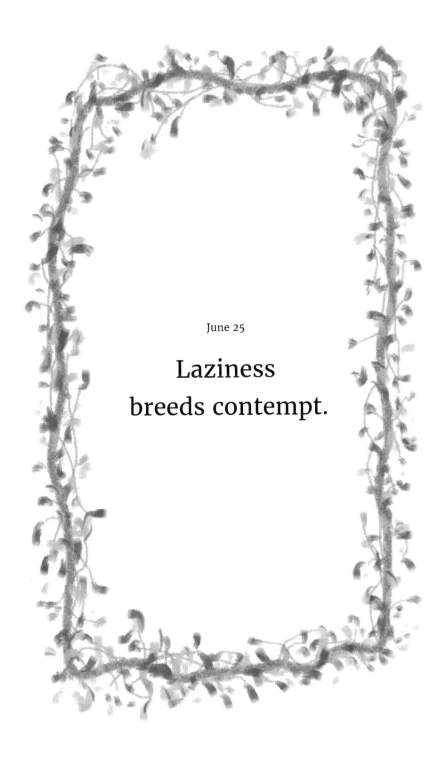

June 25

Laziness
breeds contempt.

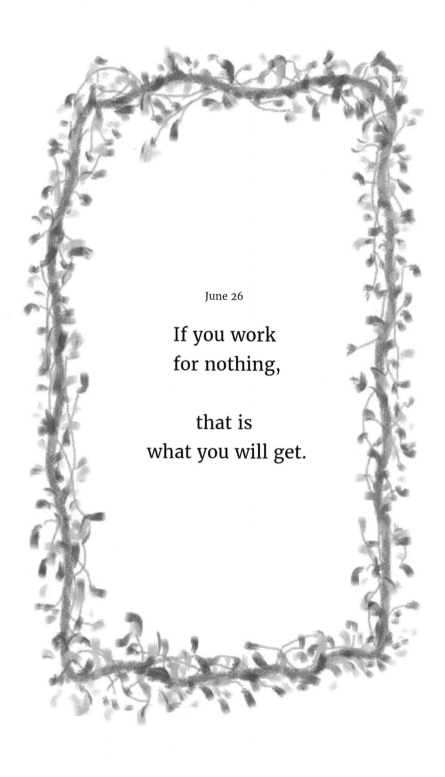

June 26

If you work
for nothing,

that is
what you will get.

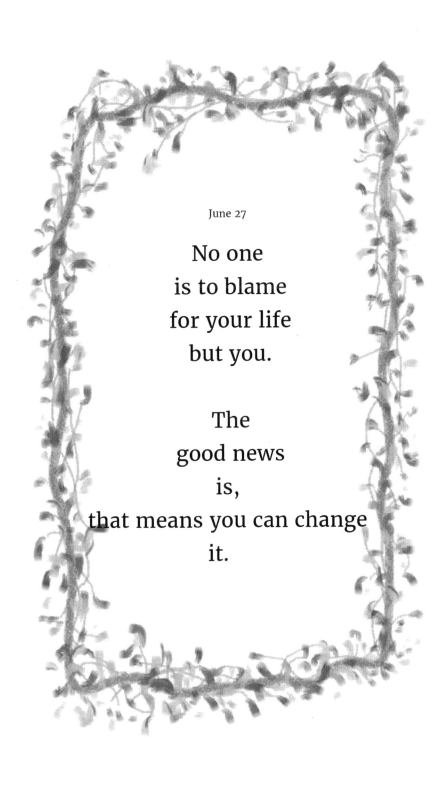

June 27

No one
is to blame
for your life
but you.

The
good news
is,
that means you can change
it.

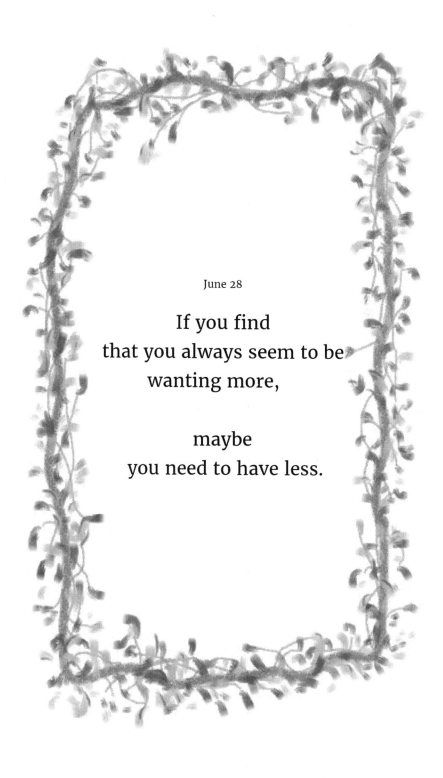

June 28

If you find
that you always seem to be
wanting more,

maybe
you need to have less.

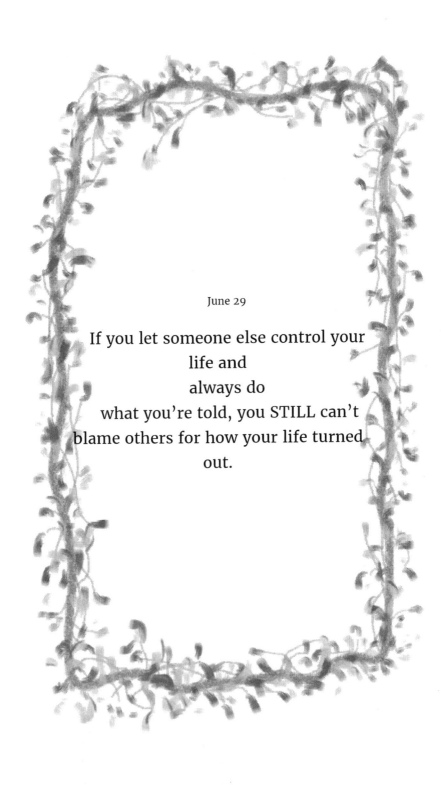

June 29

If you let someone else control your
life and
always do
what you're told, you STILL can't
blame others for how your life turned
out.

June 30

Be careful
the mistakes you make.

Some consequences last an
awfully long time.

July 1

When things
are harder,

you
appreciate them
more.

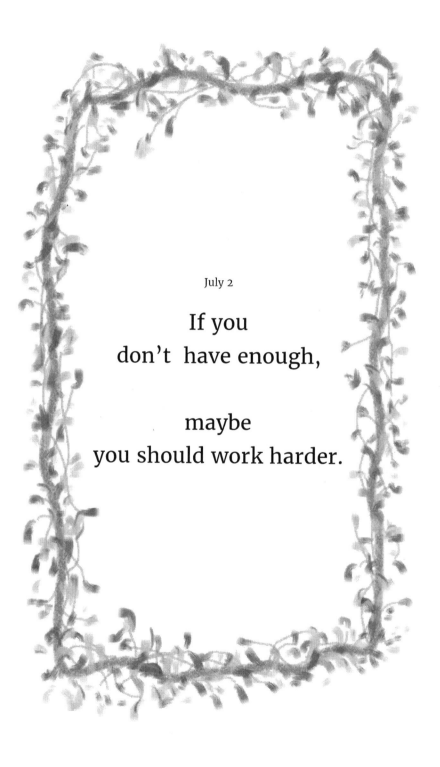

July 2

If you
don't have enough,

maybe
you should work harder.

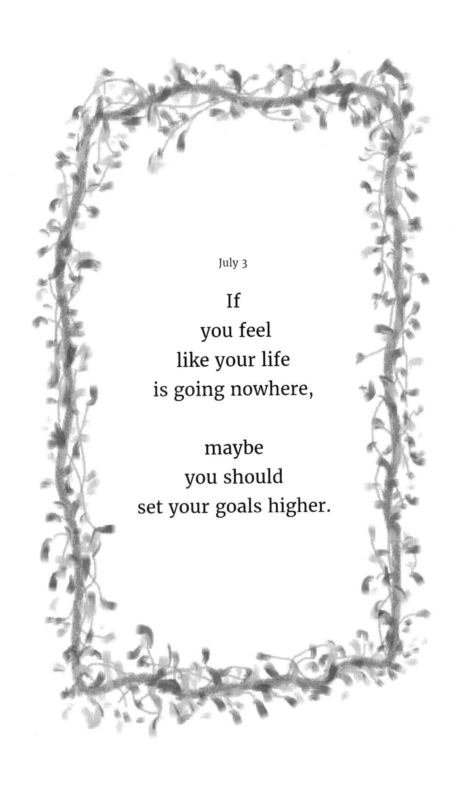

July 3

If
you feel
like your life
is going nowhere,

maybe
you should
set your goals higher.

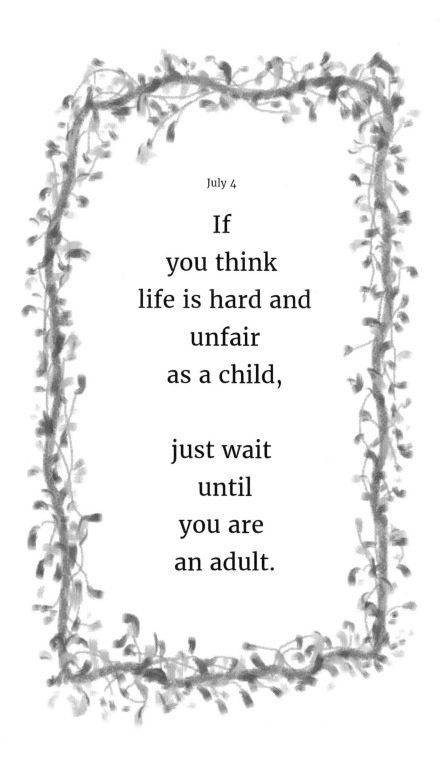

July 4

If
you think
life is hard and
unfair
as a child,

just wait
until
you are
an adult.

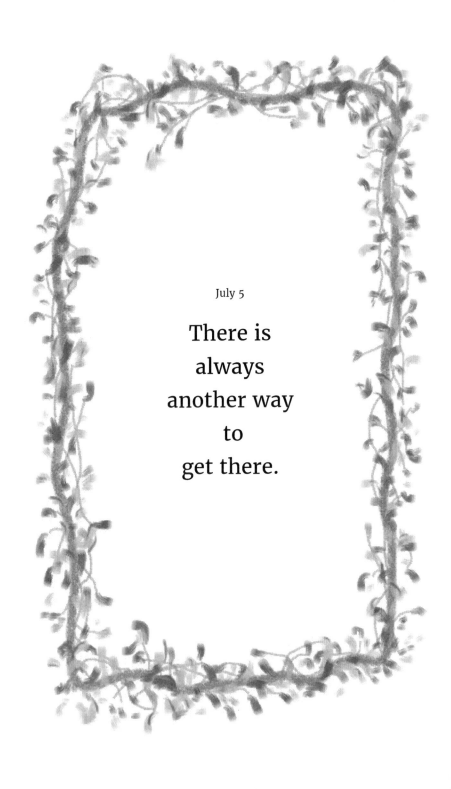

July 5

There is
always
another way
to
get there.

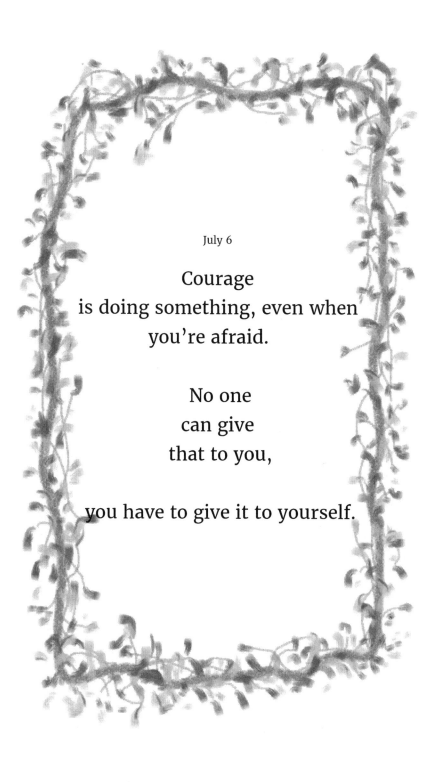

July 6

Courage
is doing something, even when
you're afraid.

No one
can give
that to you,

you have to give it to yourself.

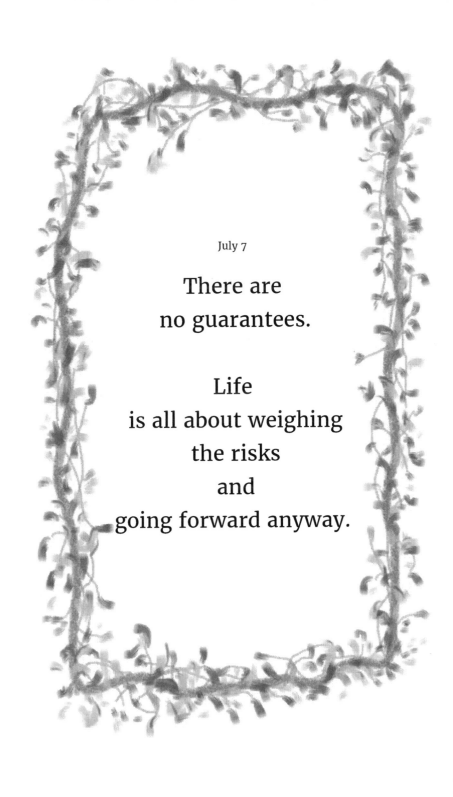

July 7

There are
no guarantees.

Life
is all about weighing
the risks
and
going forward anyway.

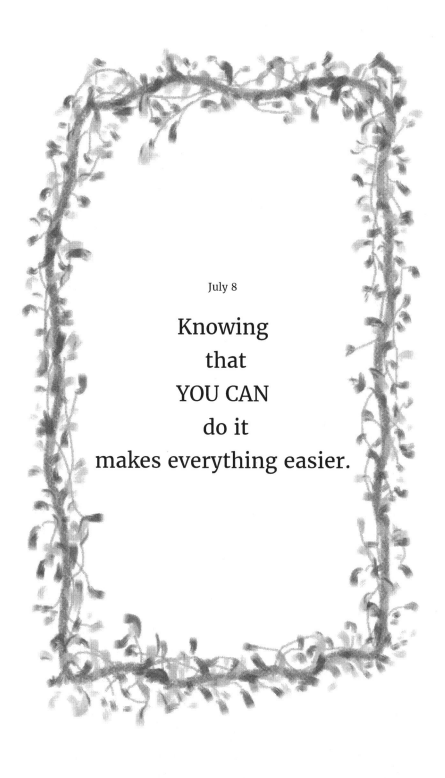

July 8

Knowing
that
YOU CAN
do it
makes everything easier.

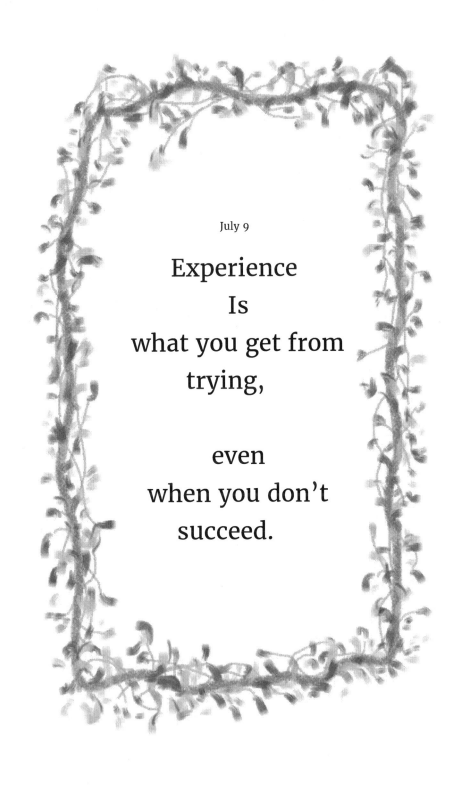

July 9

Experience
Is
what you get from
trying,

even
when you don't
succeed.

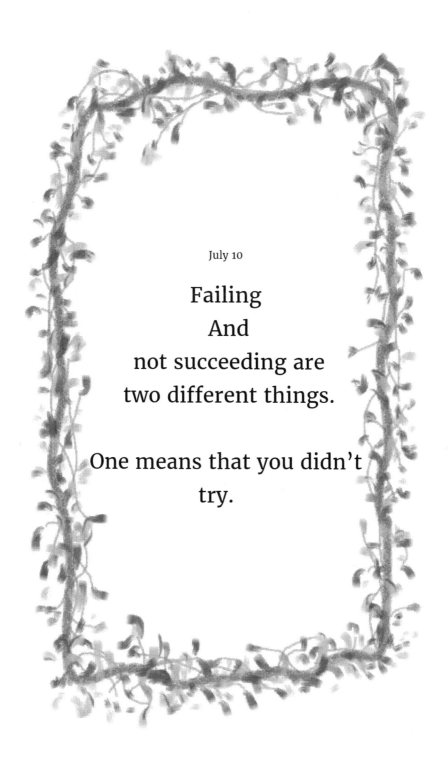

July 10

Failing
And
not succeeding are
two different things.

One means that you didn't
try.

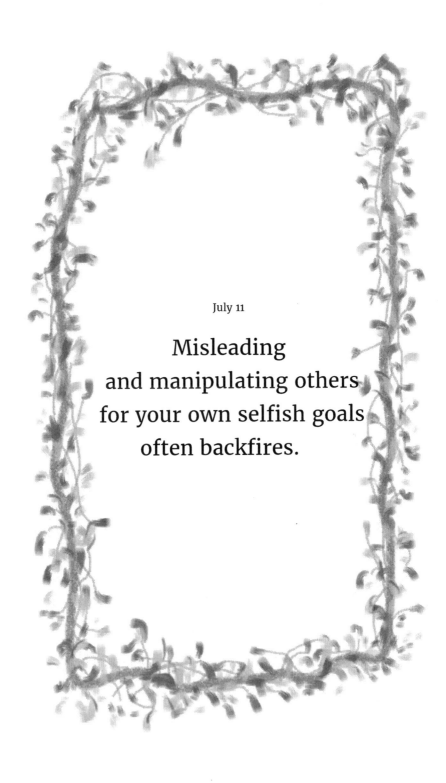

July 11

Misleading
and manipulating others
for your own selfish goals
often backfires.

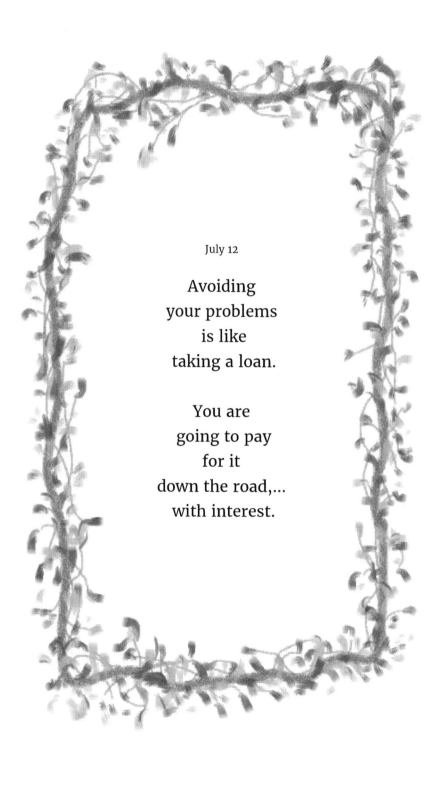

July 12

Avoiding
your problems
is like
taking a loan.

You are
going to pay
for it
down the road,...
with interest.

July 13

When you
love someone that is bad
for you,
it can be hard to leave.
But
that is what people who
respect themselves
do.

July 14

At best,
drugs help you ignore your problems
and stop caring about things that are
important to you.

It might seem fun
for a minute
but you can really pay for that in the future.

If you can't handle
your stuff now,
why make your future more difficult?

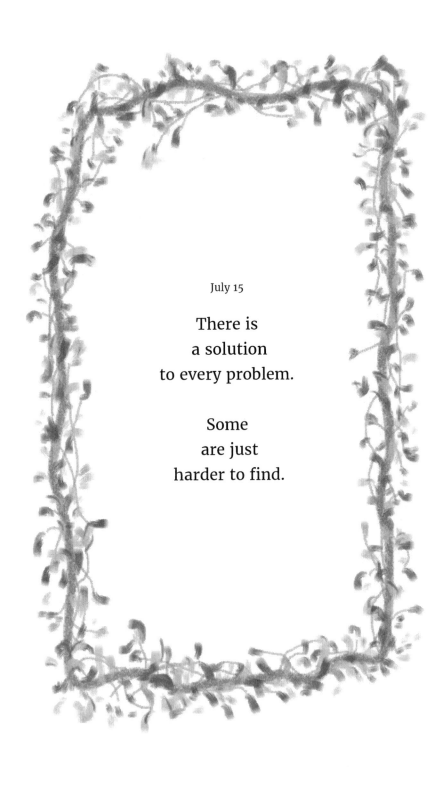

July 15

There is
a solution
to every problem.

Some
are just
harder to find.

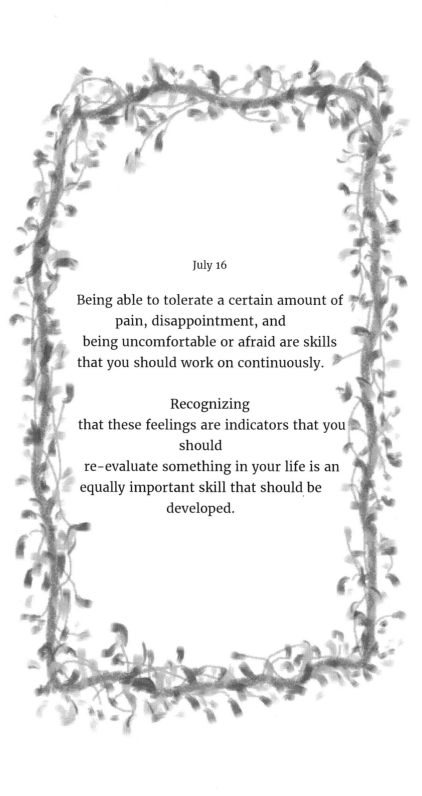

July 16

Being able to tolerate a certain amount of
pain, disappointment, and
being uncomfortable or afraid are skills
that you should work on continuously.

Recognizing
that these feelings are indicators that you
should
re-evaluate something in your life is an
equally important skill that should be
developed.

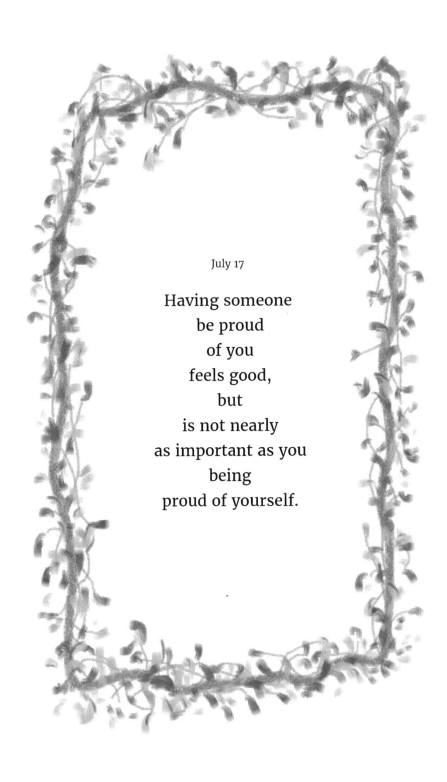

July 17

Having someone
be proud
of you
feels good,
but
is not nearly
as important as you
being
proud of yourself.

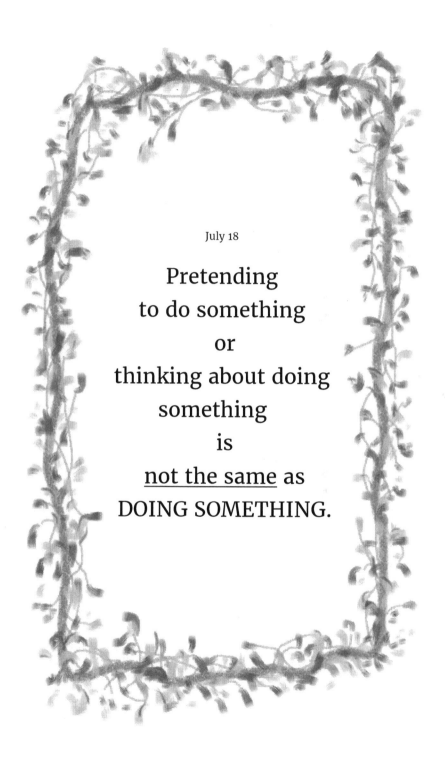

July 18

Pretending
to do something
or
thinking about doing
something
is
<u>not the same</u> as
DOING SOMETHING.

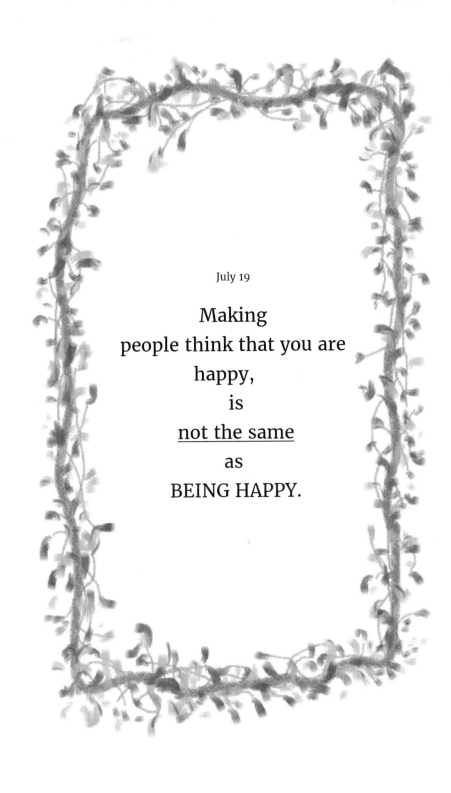

July 19

Making
people think that you are
happy,
is
<u>not the same</u>
as
BEING HAPPY.

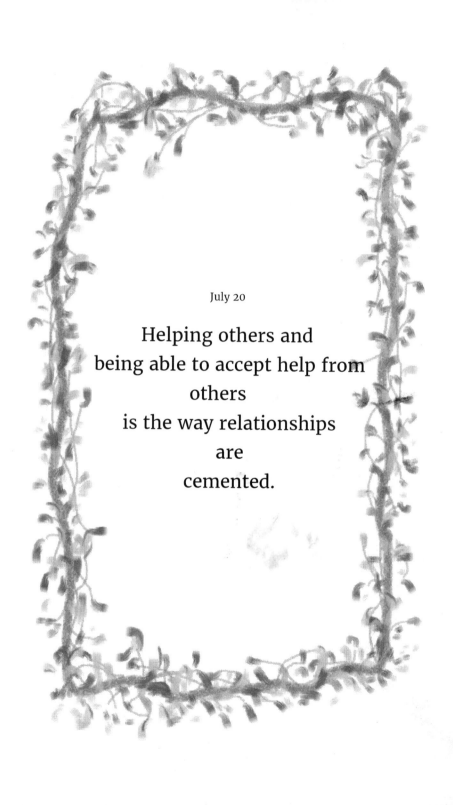

July 20

Helping others and
being able to accept help from
others
is the way relationships
are
cemented.

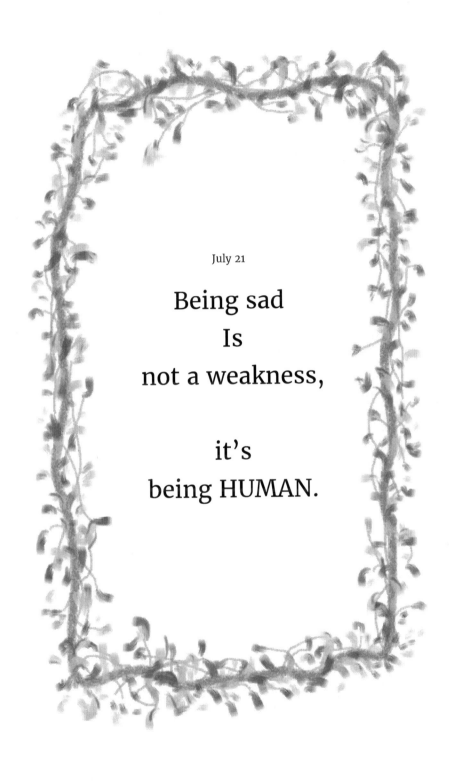

July 21

Being sad
Is
not a weakness,

it's
being HUMAN.

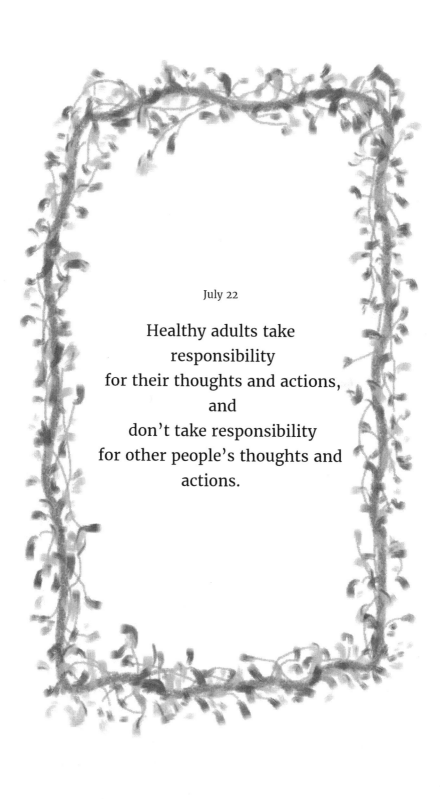

July 22

Healthy adults take
responsibility
for their thoughts and actions,
and
don't take responsibility
for other people's thoughts and
actions.

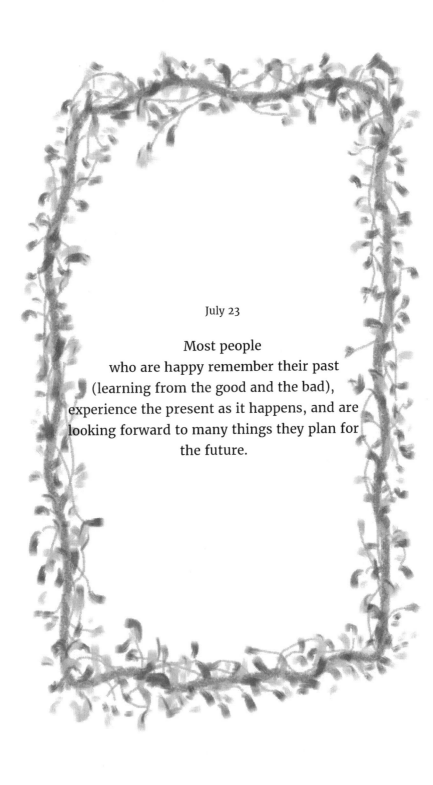

July 23

Most people
who are happy remember their past
(learning from the good and the bad),
experience the present as it happens, and are
looking forward to many things they plan for
the future.

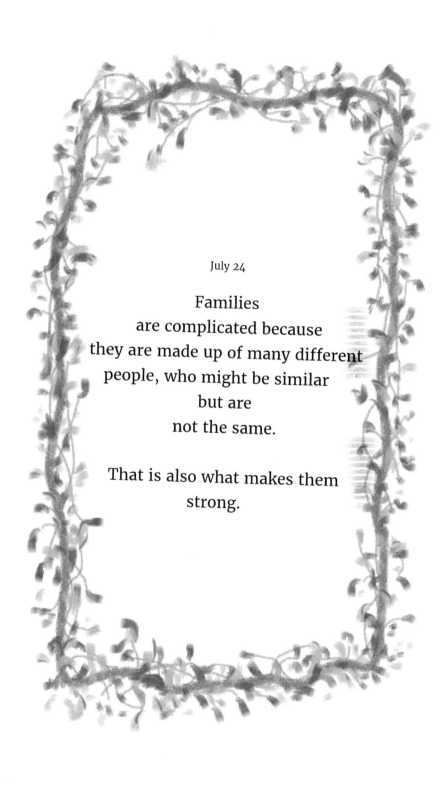

July 24

Families
are complicated because
they are made up of many different
people, who might be similar
but are
not the same.

That is also what makes them
strong.

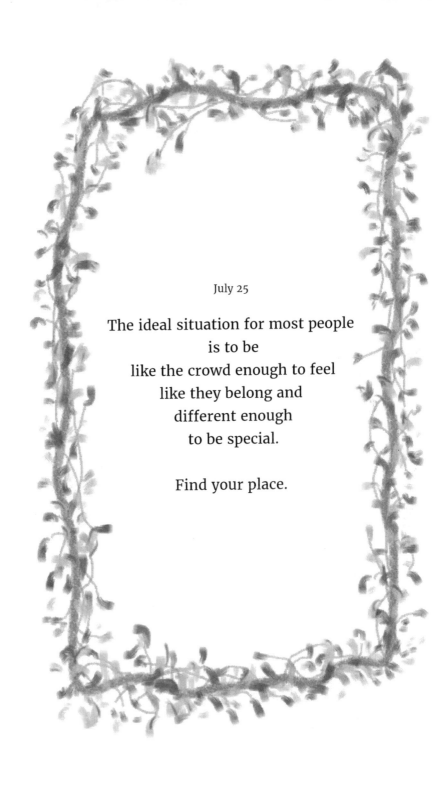

July 25

The ideal situation for most people
is to be
like the crowd enough to feel
like they belong and
different enough
to be special.

Find your place.

July 26

Strange
is funny
and
interesting.

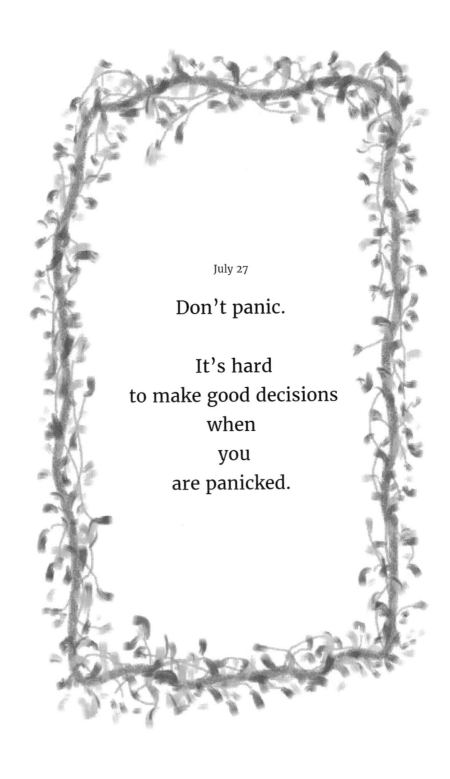

July 27

Don't panic.

It's hard
to make good decisions
when
you
are panicked.

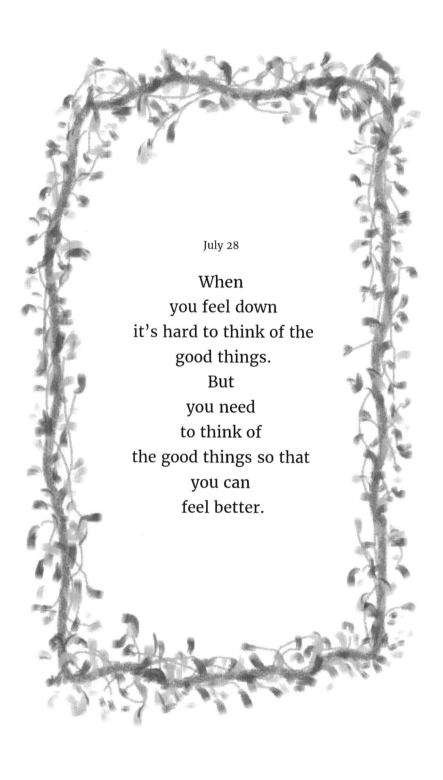

July 28

When
you feel down
it's hard to think of the
good things.
But
you need
to think of
the good things so that
you can
feel better.

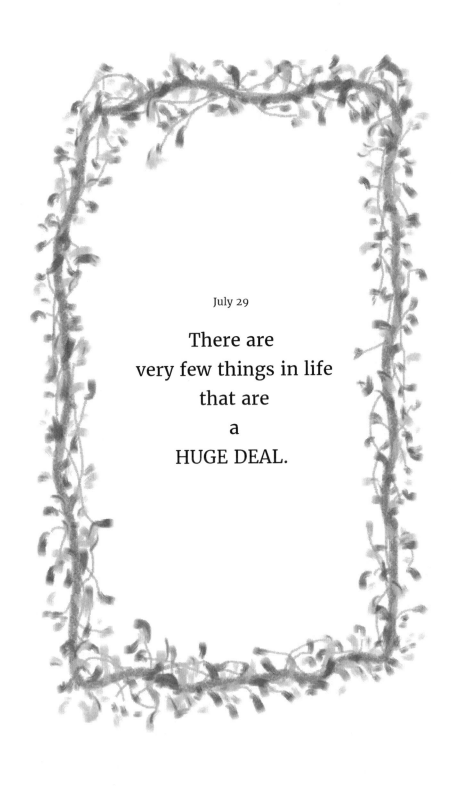

July 29

There are
very few things in life
that are
a
HUGE DEAL.

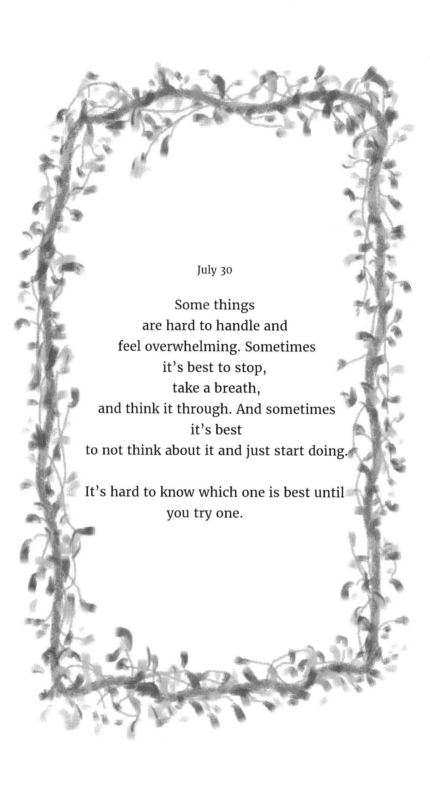

July 30

Some things
are hard to handle and
feel overwhelming. Sometimes
it's best to stop,
take a breath,
and think it through. And sometimes
it's best
to not think about it and just start doing.

It's hard to know which one is best until
you try one.

July 31

Sometimes someone
sounds like a friend, acts like a friend,
feels like a friend until you find out that
that person
is not a friend
and
that hurts.

August 1

Sometimes you
have to
find your own way.

August 2

Nothing is forever.

August 3

Tomorrow you can start over.

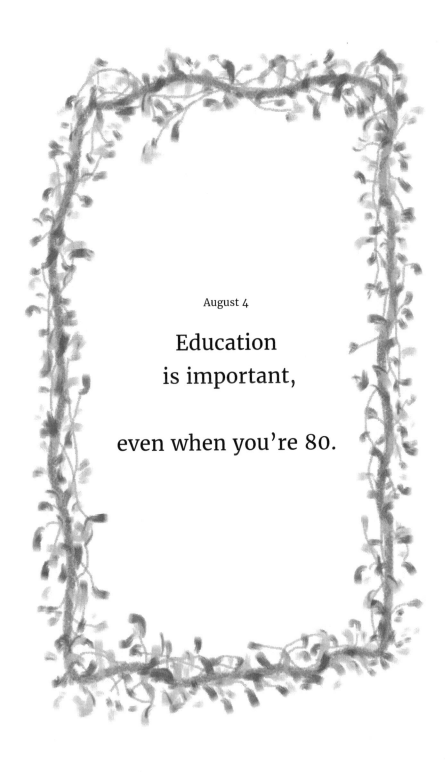

August 4

Education
is important,

even when you're 80.

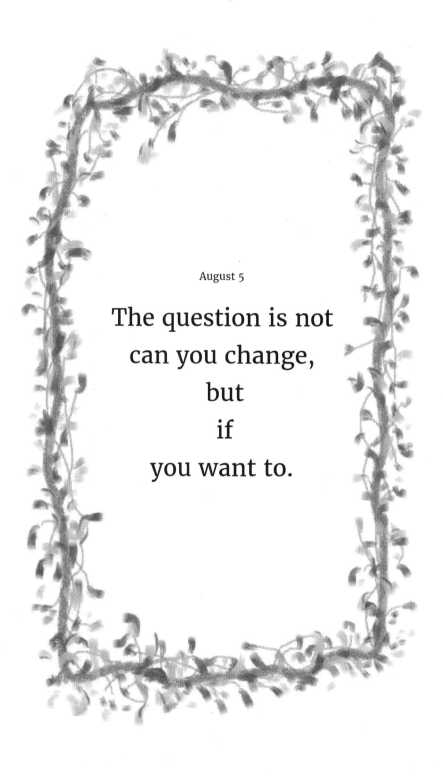

August 5

The question is not

can you change,

but

if

you want to.

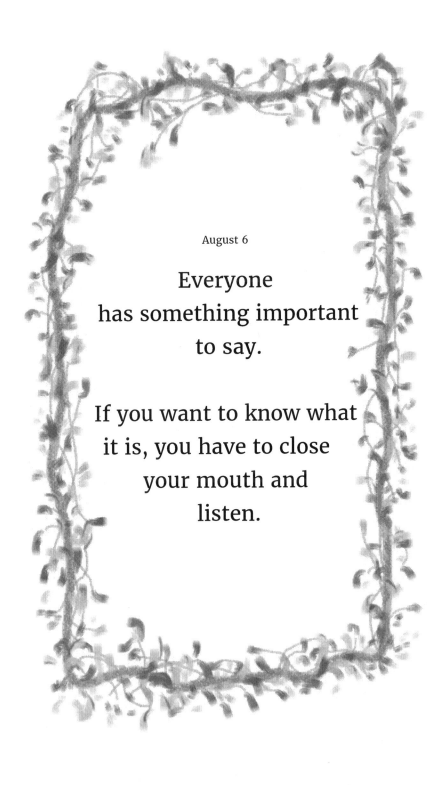

August 6

Everyone
has something important
to say.

If you want to know what
it is, you have to close
your mouth and
listen.

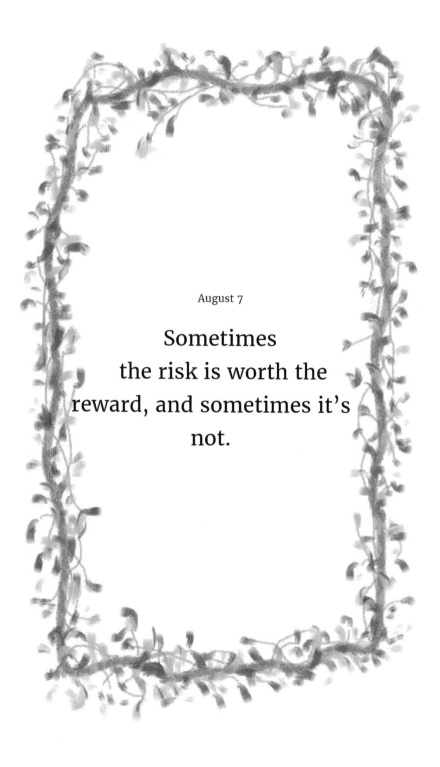

August 7

Sometimes
the risk is worth the
reward, and sometimes it's
not.

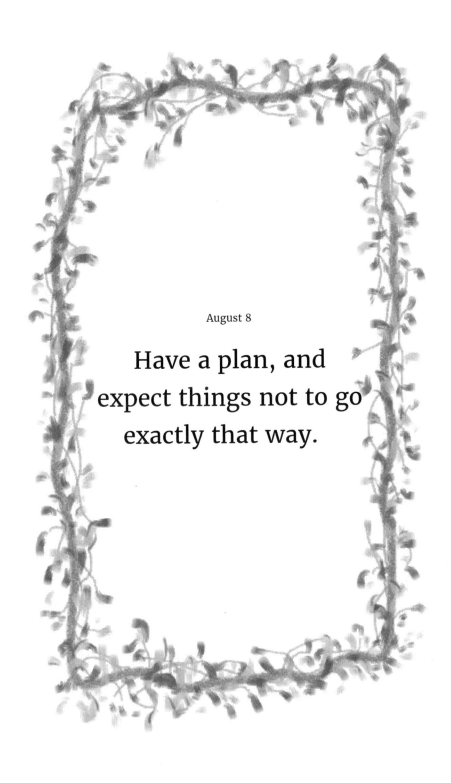

August 8

Have a plan, and
expect things not to go
exactly that way.

August 9

Giving gifts is not as important as listening.

August 10

If you care about someone,
be aware
of how
they feel
and
what's important
to them.

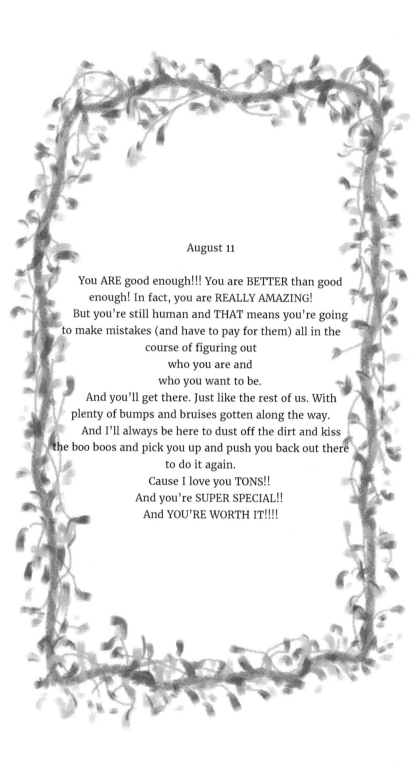

August 11

You ARE good enough!!! You are BETTER than good
enough! In fact, you are REALLY AMAZING!
But you're still human and THAT means you're going
to make mistakes (and have to pay for them) all in the
course of figuring out
who you are and
who you want to be.
And you'll get there. Just like the rest of us. With
plenty of bumps and bruises gotten along the way.
And I'll always be here to dust off the dirt and kiss
the boo boos and pick you up and push you back out there
to do it again.
Cause I love you TONS!!
And you're SUPER SPECIAL!!
And YOU'RE WORTH IT!!!!

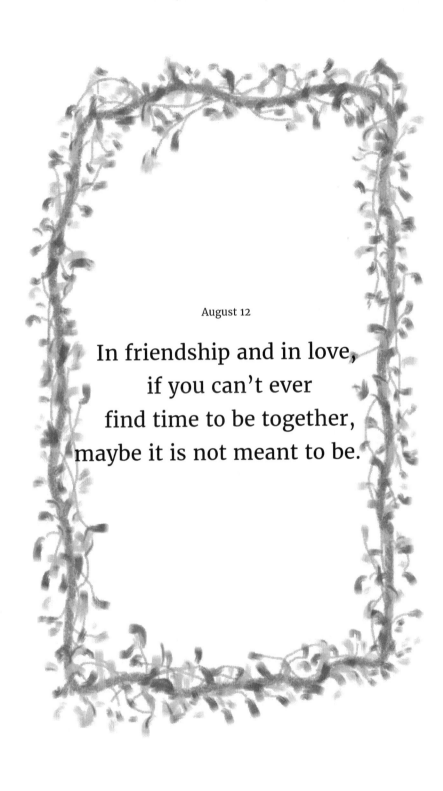

August 12

In friendship and in love,
if you can't ever
find time to be together,
maybe it is not meant to be.

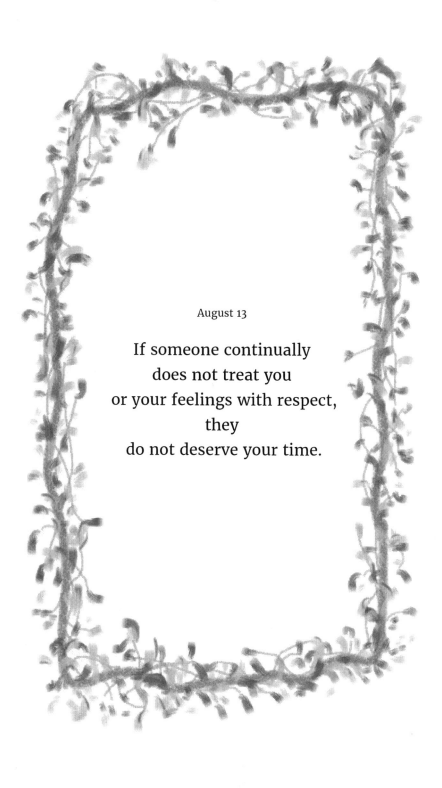

August 13

If someone continually
does not treat you
or your feelings with respect,
they
do not deserve your time.

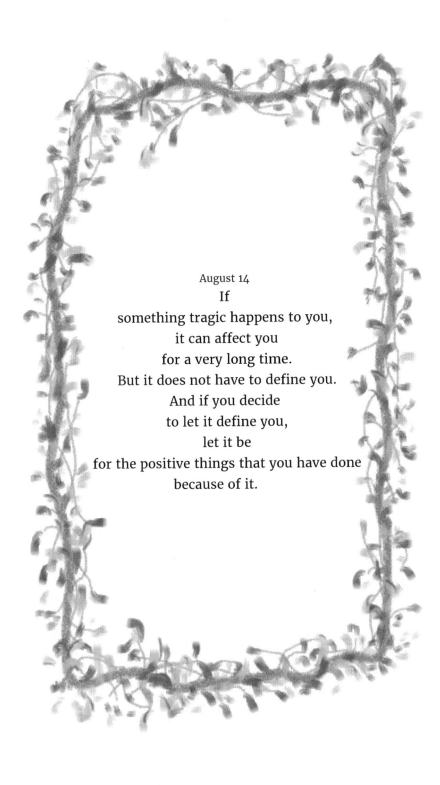

August 14

If
something tragic happens to you,
it can affect you
for a very long time.
But it does not have to define you.
And if you decide
to let it define you,
let it be
for the positive things that you have done
because of it.

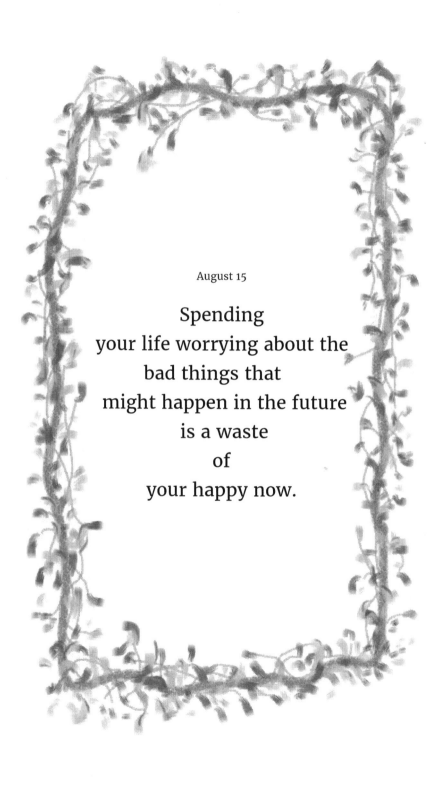

August 15

Spending
your life worrying about the
bad things that
might happen in the future
is a waste
of
your happy now.

August 16

Good things happen.
Bad things happen.

Only you
can make it
a
big deal.

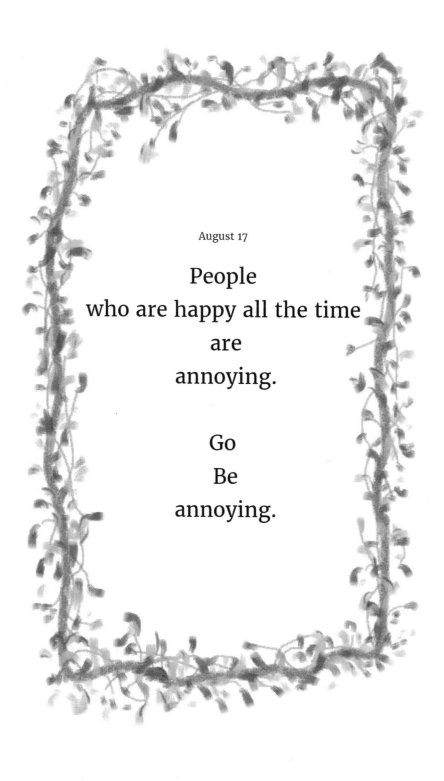

August 17

People
who are happy all the time
are
annoying.

Go
Be
annoying.

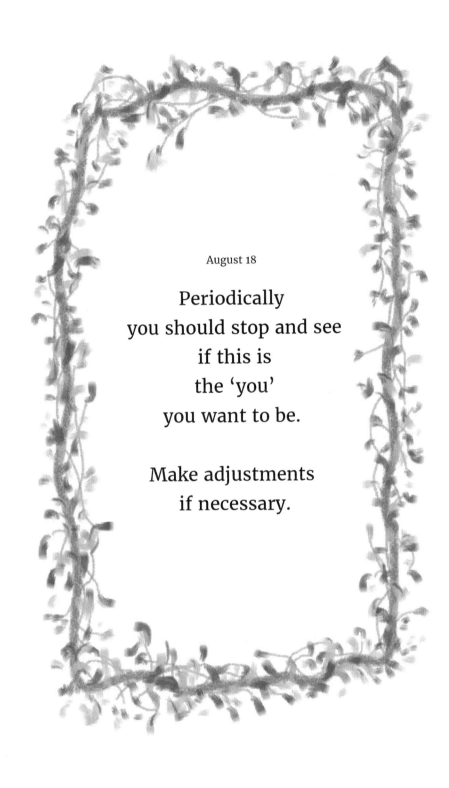

August 18

Periodically
you should stop and see
if this is
the 'you'
you want to be.

Make adjustments
if necessary.

August 19

Relationships are not
equal.

Find
a balance
you
enjoy living with.

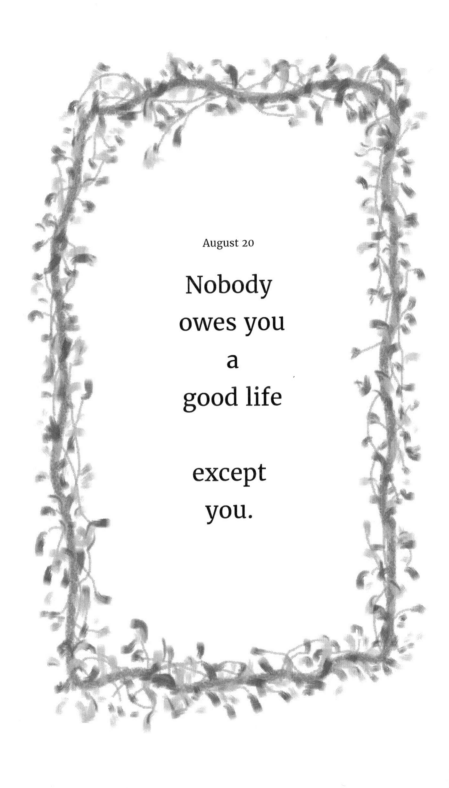

August 20

Nobody
owes you
a
good life

except
you.

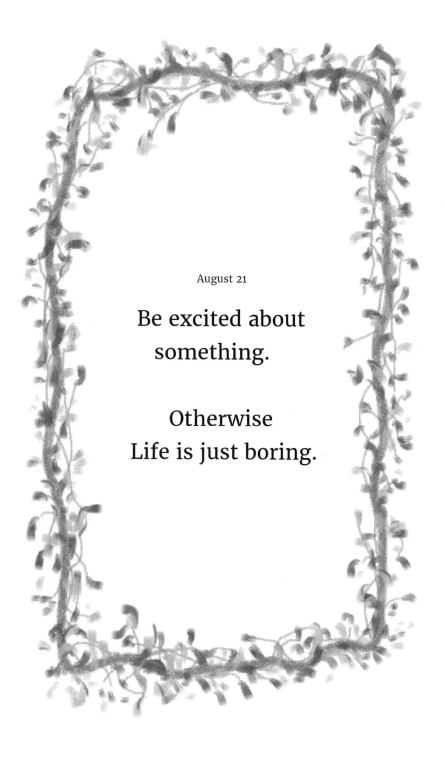

August 21

Be excited about
something.

Otherwise
Life is just boring.

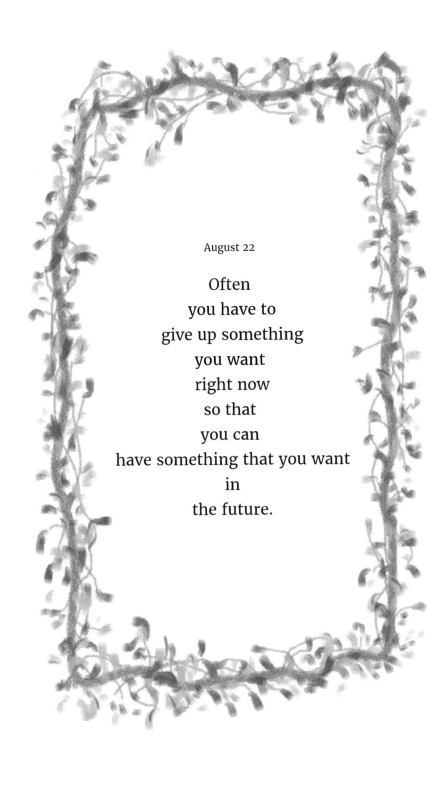

August 22

Often
you have to
give up something
you want
right now
so that
you can
have something that you want
in
the future.

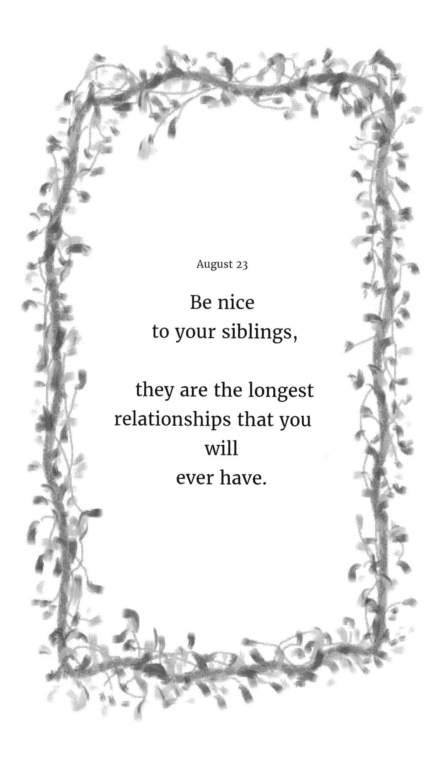

August 23

Be nice
to your siblings,

they are the longest
relationships that you
will
ever have.

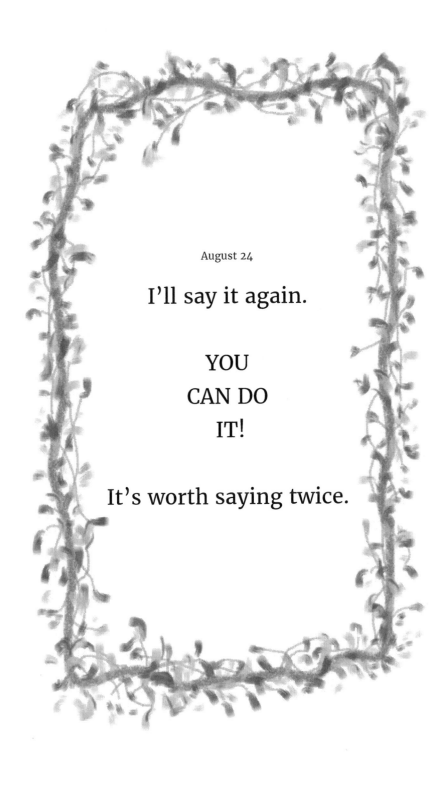

August 24

I'll say it again.

YOU
CAN DO
IT!

It's worth saying twice.

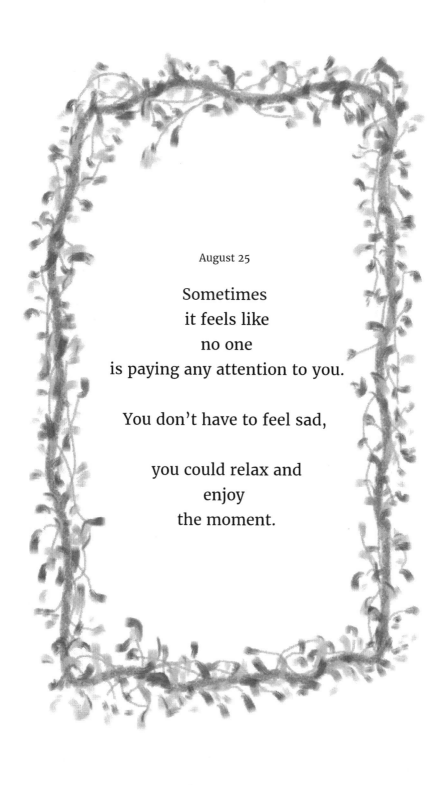

August 25

Sometimes
it feels like
no one
is paying any attention to you.

You don't have to feel sad,

you could relax and
enjoy
the moment.

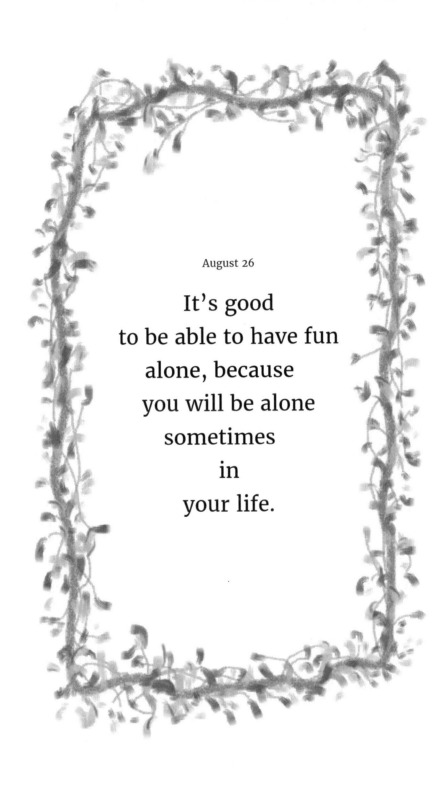

August 26

It's good
to be able to have fun
alone, because
you will be alone
sometimes
in
your life.

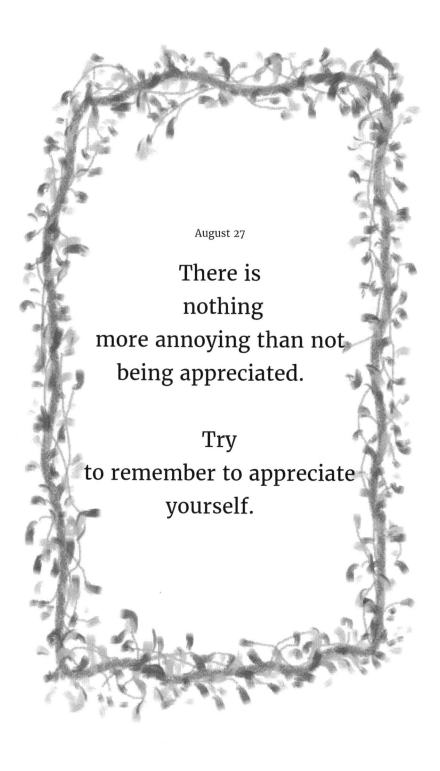

August 27

There is
nothing
more annoying than not
being appreciated.

Try
to remember to appreciate
yourself.

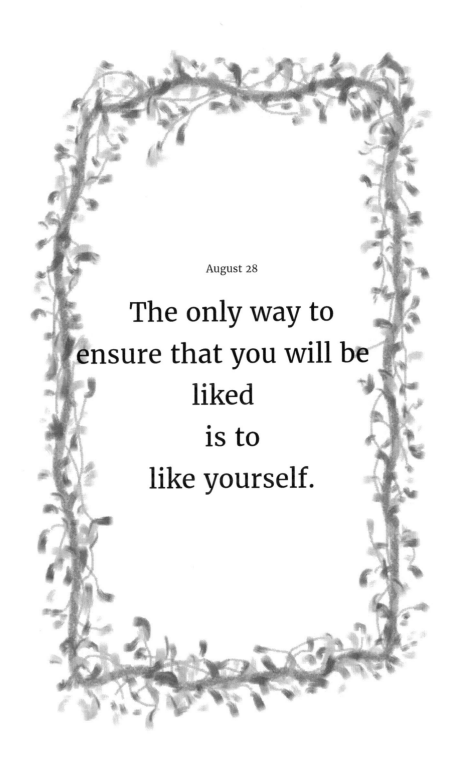

August 28

The only way to
ensure that you will be
liked
is to
like yourself.

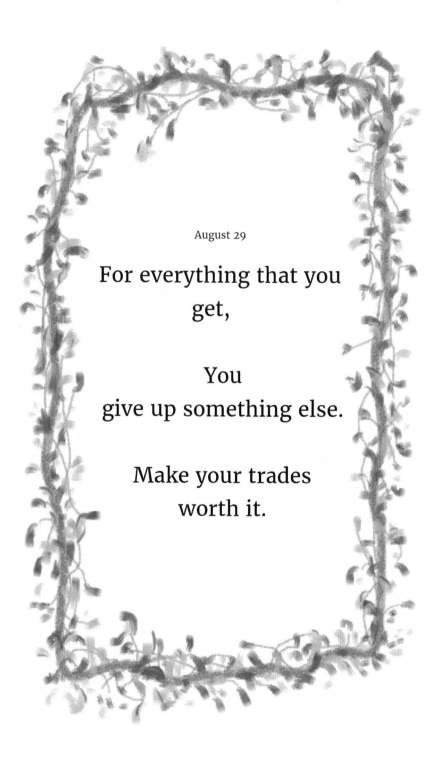

August 29

For everything that you
get,

You
give up something else.

Make your trades
worth it.

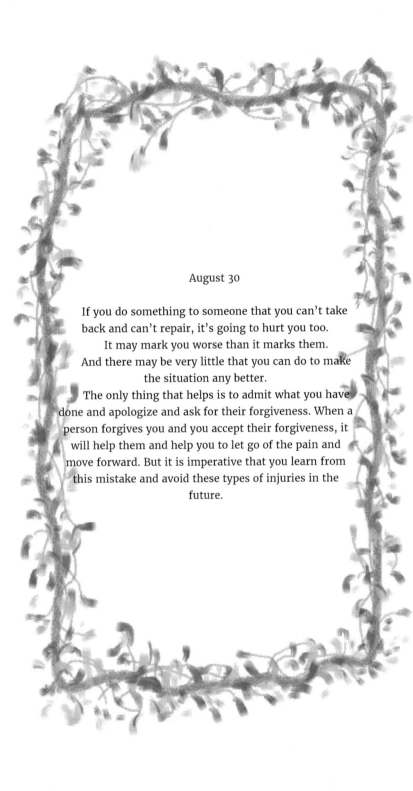

August 30

If you do something to someone that you can't take
back and can't repair, it's going to hurt you too.
It may mark you worse than it marks them.
And there may be very little that you can do to make
the situation any better.
The only thing that helps is to admit what you have
done and apologize and ask for their forgiveness. When a
person forgives you and you accept their forgiveness, it
will help them and help you to let go of the pain and
move forward. But it is imperative that you learn from
this mistake and avoid these types of injuries in the
future.

August 31

Just
because
they do it
on tv,
does not
make
it
acceptable behavior.

September 1

If you are standing near someone
who is doing something bad,
odds are
the bad
will spill over onto you, whether
you participate
or not,
whether
they are your friend
or not.

September 2

Funny on tv
is not necessarily funny
in real life.

September 3

Lots of responsibilities are disguised as privileges.

September 4

Sometimes
you will
need to hear
"I love you" and
no one
will say it.

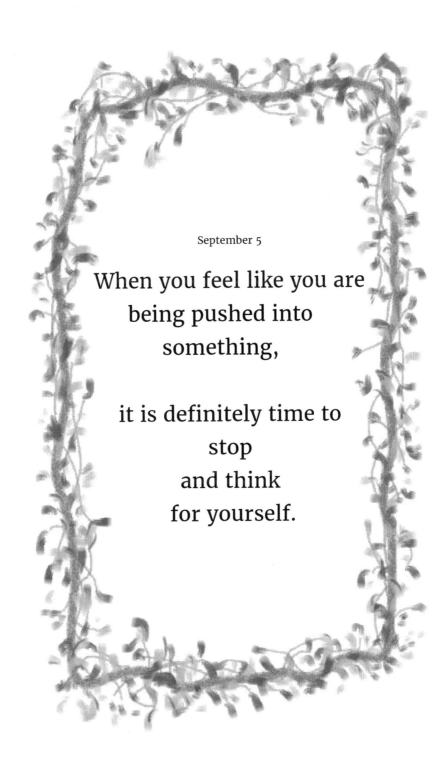

September 5

When you feel like you are
being pushed into
something,

it is definitely time to
stop
and think
for yourself.

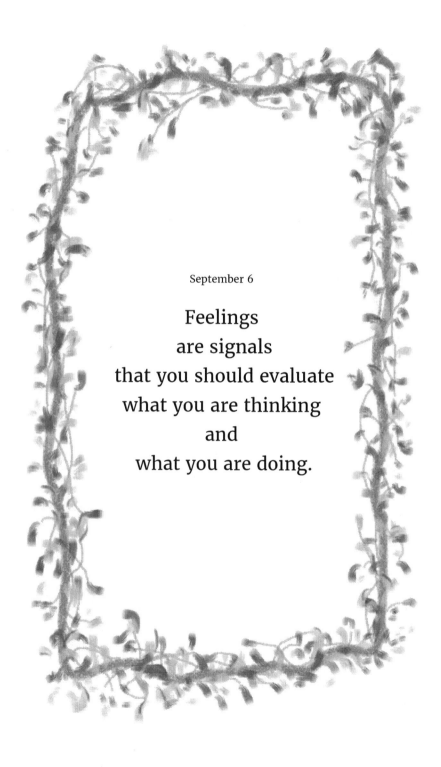

September 6

Feelings
are signals
that you should evaluate
what you are thinking
and
what you are doing.

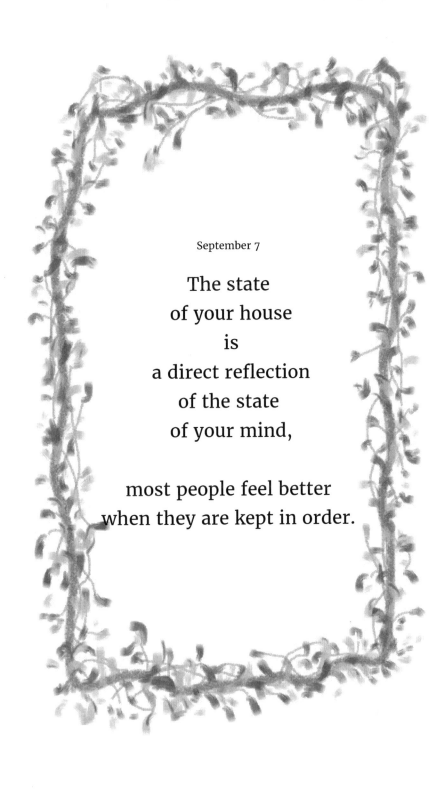

September 7

The state
of your house
is
a direct reflection
of the state
of your mind,

most people feel better
when they are kept in order.

September 8

Skirting
your obligations can be
done,

but it
won't
make you feel good.

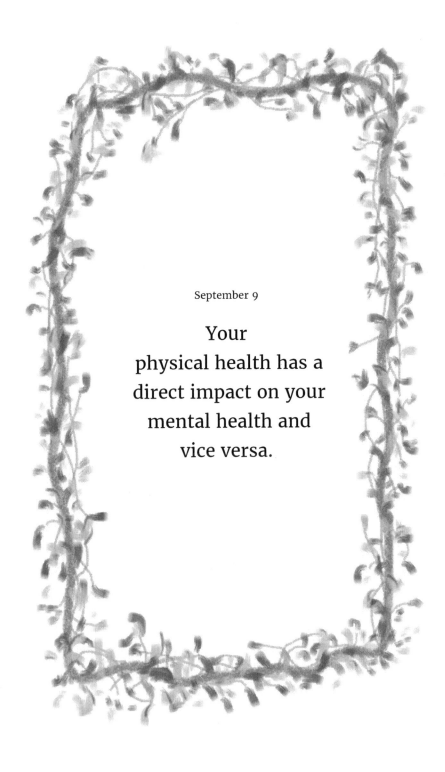

September 9

Your
physical health has a
direct impact on your
mental health and
vice versa.

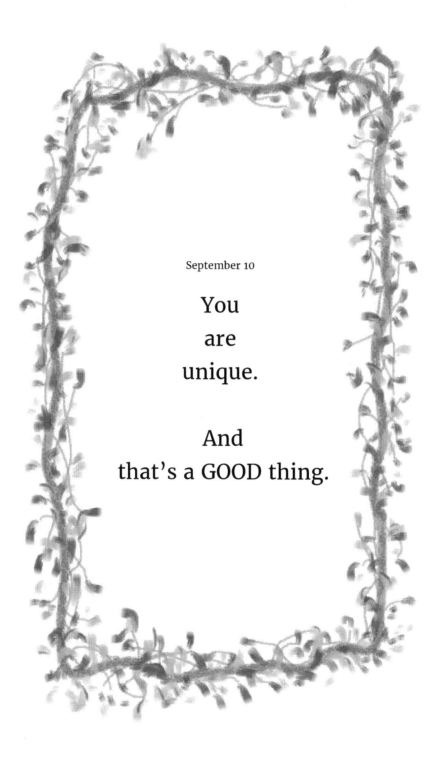

September 10

You
are
unique.

And
that's a GOOD thing.

September 11

Everyone has problems.

You are not alone.

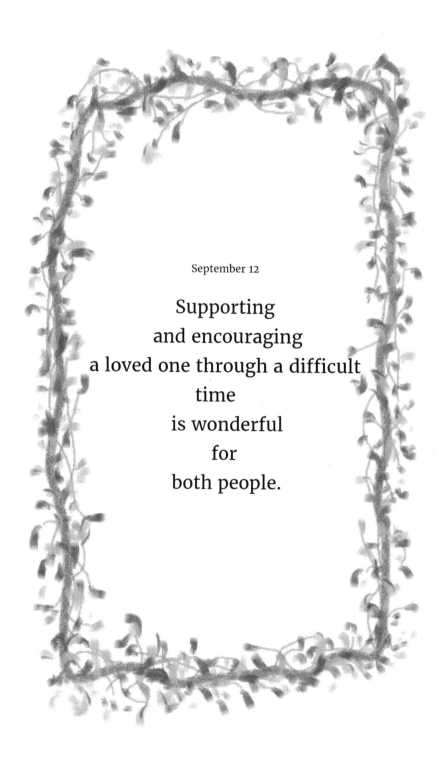

September 12

Supporting
and encouraging
a loved one through a difficult
time
is wonderful
for
both people.

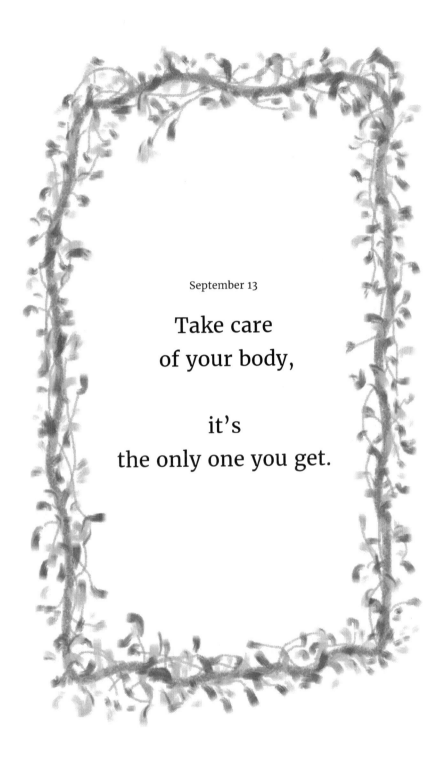

September 13

Take care
of your body,

it's
the only one you get.

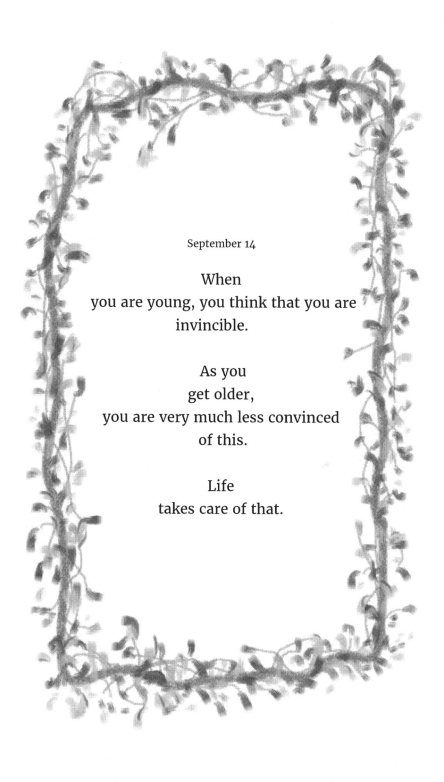

September 14

When
you are young, you think that you are
invincible.

As you
get older,
you are very much less convinced
of this.

Life
takes care of that.

September 15

Sometimes
your children will not meet their
challenges
and it will hurt (them and you).

Don't fix it for them and deny them
that learning experience.

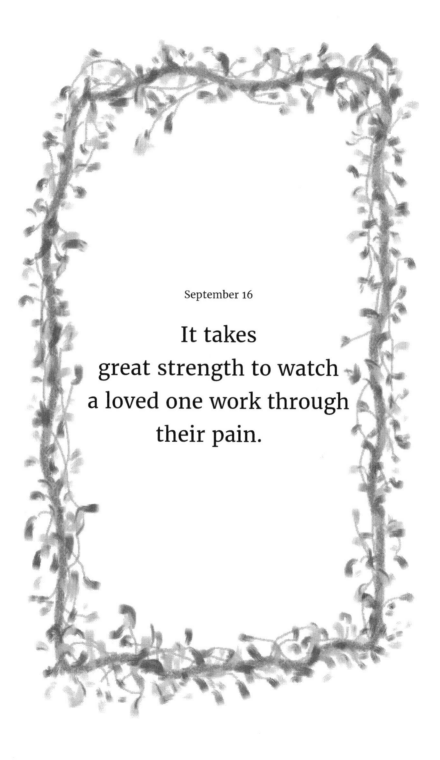

September 16

It takes
great strength to watch
a loved one work through
their pain.

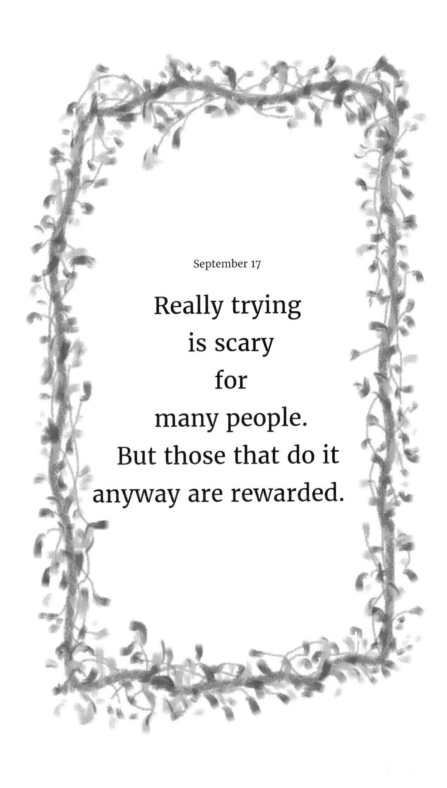

September 17

Really trying
is scary
for
many people.
But those that do it
anyway are rewarded.

September 18

Sometimes
the rewards
are not
the ones you expected.
But they are still rewards.

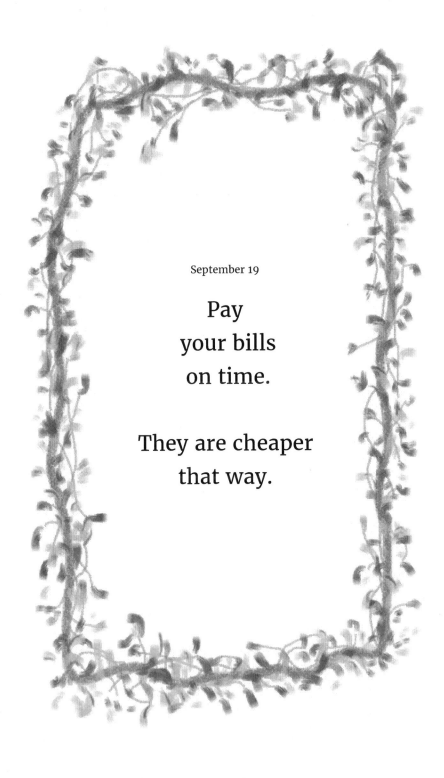

September 19

Pay
your bills
on time.

They are cheaper
that way.

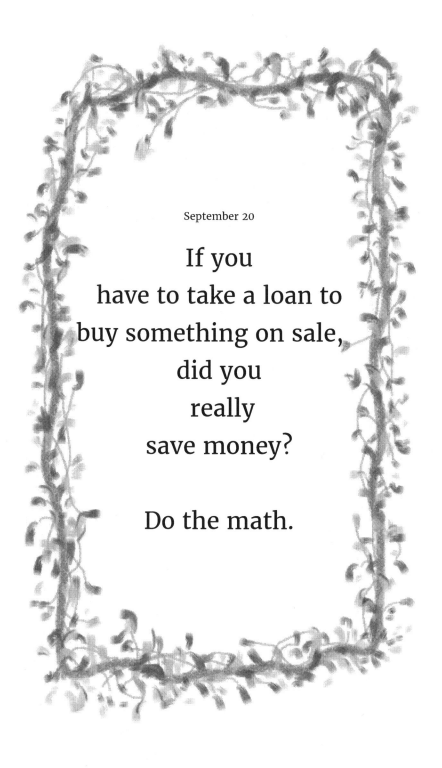

September 20

If you
have to take a loan to
buy something on sale,
did you
really
save money?

Do the math.

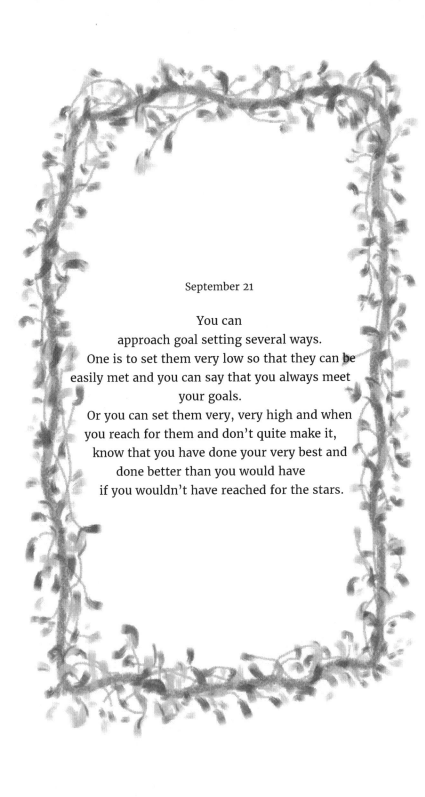

September 21

You can
approach goal setting several ways.
One is to set them very low so that they can be
easily met and you can say that you always meet
your goals.
Or you can set them very, very high and when
you reach for them and don't quite make it,
know that you have done your very best and
done better than you would have
if you wouldn't have reached for the stars.

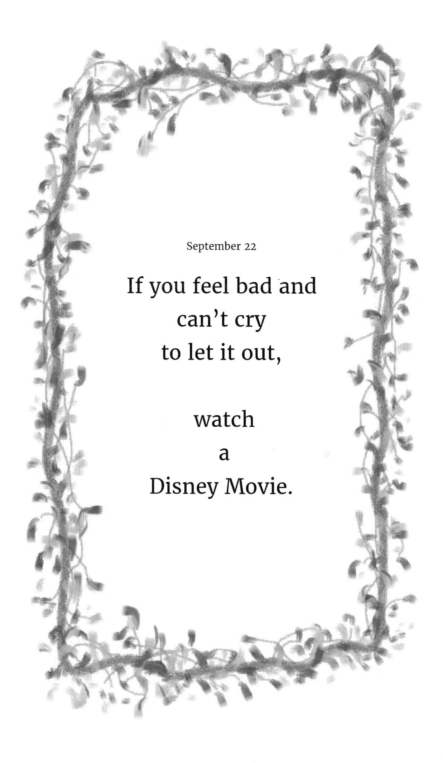

September 22

If you feel bad and
can't cry
to let it out,

watch

a

Disney Movie.

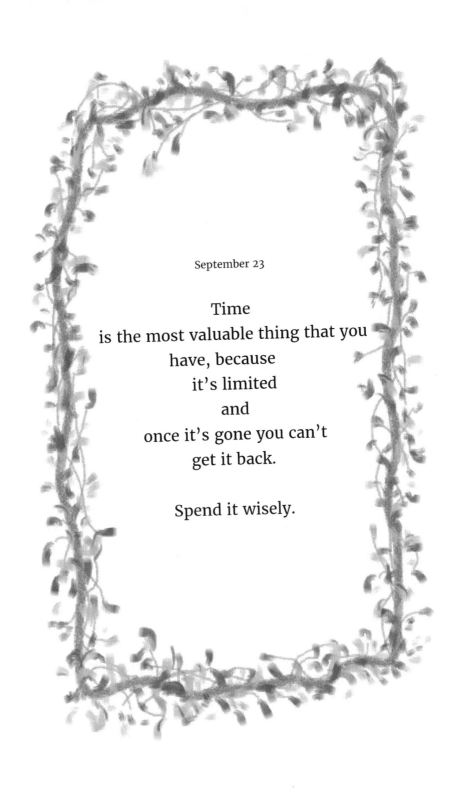

September 23

Time
is the most valuable thing that you
have, because
it's limited
and
once it's gone you can't
get it back.

Spend it wisely.

September 24

Being angry can be a great motivator to DO SOMETHING ABOUT IT.

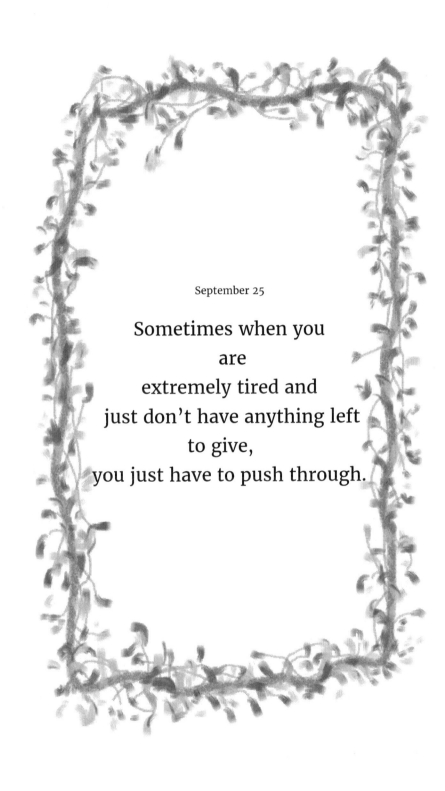

September 25

Sometimes when you
are
extremely tired and
just don't have anything left
to give,
you just have to push through.

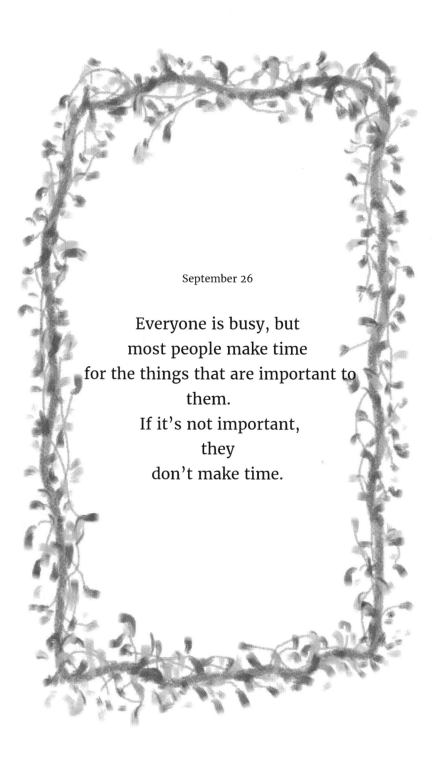

September 26

Everyone is busy, but
most people make time
for the things that are important to
them.
If it's not important,
they
don't make time.

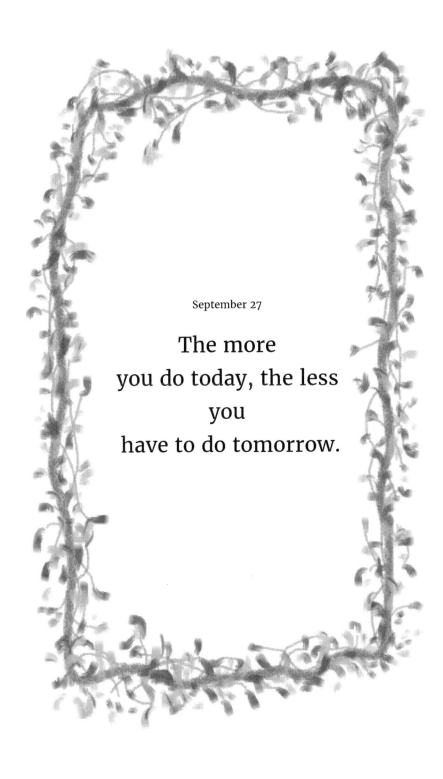

September 27

The more
you do today, the less
you
have to do tomorrow.

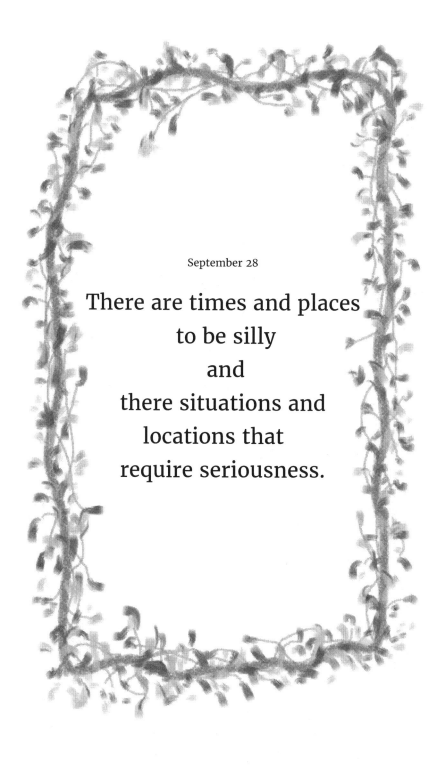

September 28

There are times and places
to be silly
and
there situations and
locations that
require seriousness.

September 29

Sometimes you will get
more done
if you take a rest first,
and
sometimes work
has to
come first.

September 30

Procrastination
is short term avoidance
and
it makes
life harder
in
the long run.

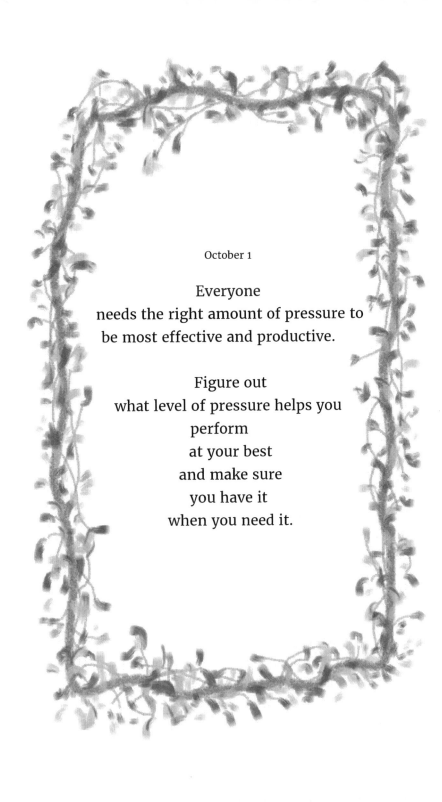

October 1

Everyone
needs the right amount of pressure to
be most effective and productive.

Figure out
what level of pressure helps you
perform
at your best
and make sure
you have it
when you need it.

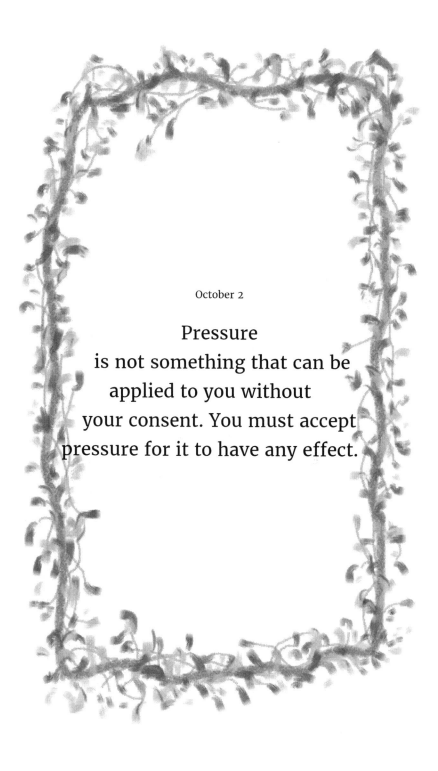

October 2

Pressure
is not something that can be
applied to you without
your consent. You must accept
pressure for it to have any effect.

October 3

Only children
tell their loved ones where they are
and when they will be home because
they have to.
Adults
do it
because they are considerate, mature
adults.

October 4

A single lie
can erase
a
thousand
truths
you've told.

October 5

No one
Likes
a tattle-tale
or
a secretive sneak.

Find the ground that lies
between.

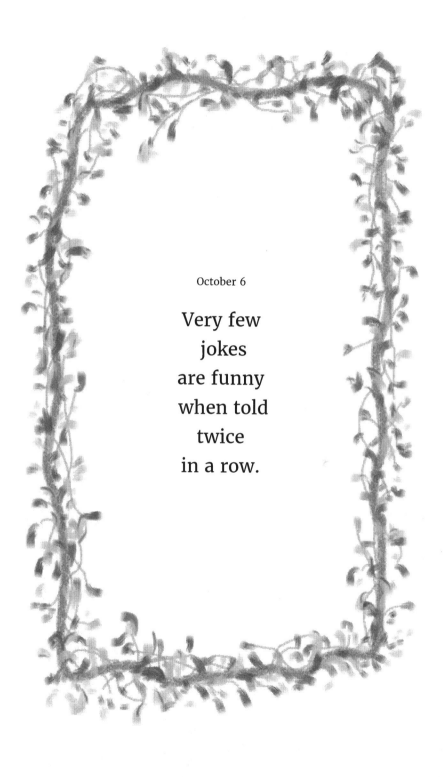

October 6

Very few
jokes
are funny
when told
twice
in a row.

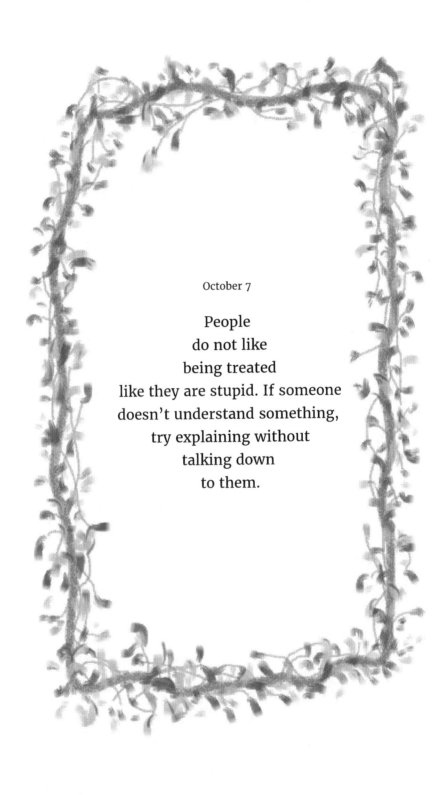

October 7

People
do not like
being treated
like they are stupid. If someone
doesn't understand something,
try explaining without
talking down
to them.

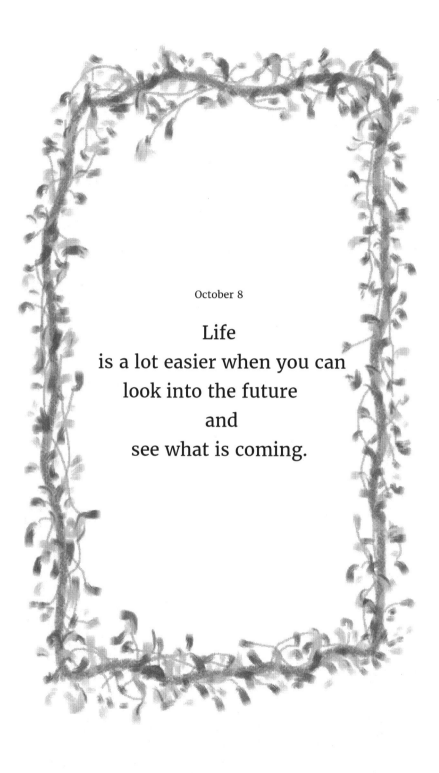

October 8

Life
is a lot easier when you can
look into the future
and
see what is coming.

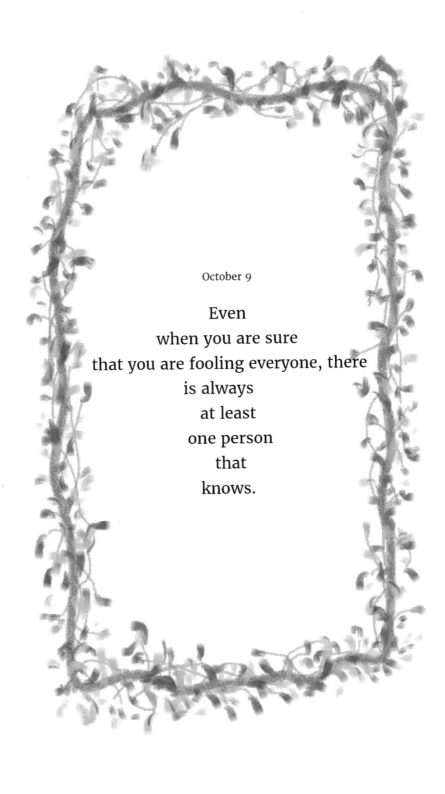

October 9

Even
when you are sure
that you are fooling everyone, there
is always
at least
one person
that
knows.

October 10

Tell
your loved ones that
you love them every day.

You can never be sure
when you will see them again.

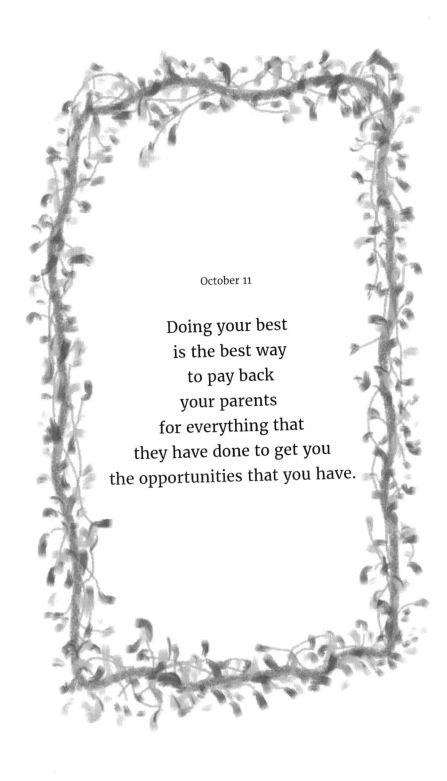

October 11

Doing your best
is the best way
to pay back
your parents
for everything that
they have done to get you
the opportunities that you have.

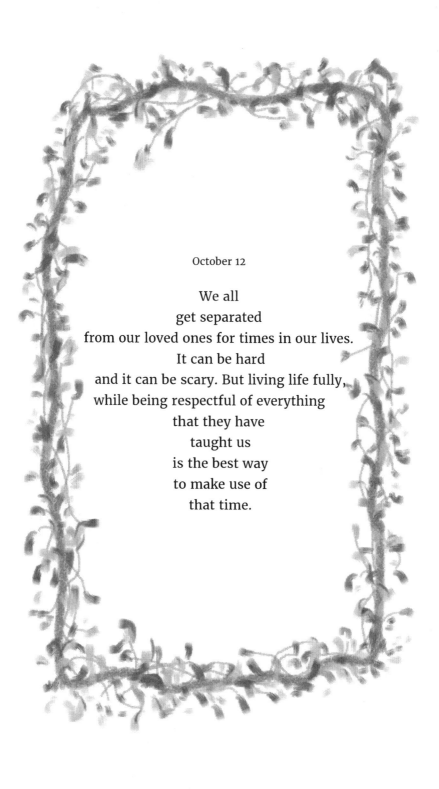

October 12

We all
get separated
from our loved ones for times in our lives.
It can be hard
and it can be scary. But living life fully,
while being respectful of everything
that they have
taught us
is the best way
to make use of
that time.

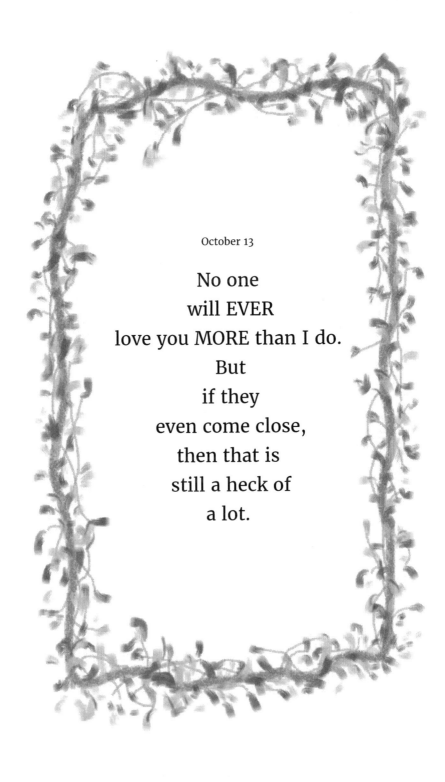

October 13

No one
will EVER
love you MORE than I do.
But
if they
even come close,
then that is
still a heck of
a lot.

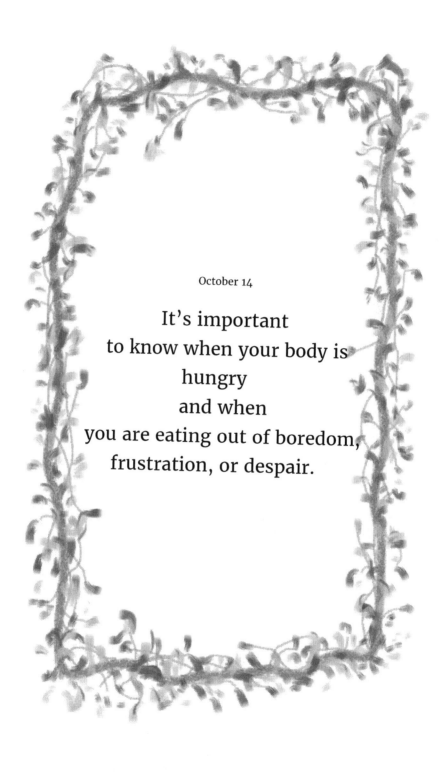

October 14

It's important
to know when your body is
hungry
and when
you are eating out of boredom,
frustration, or despair.

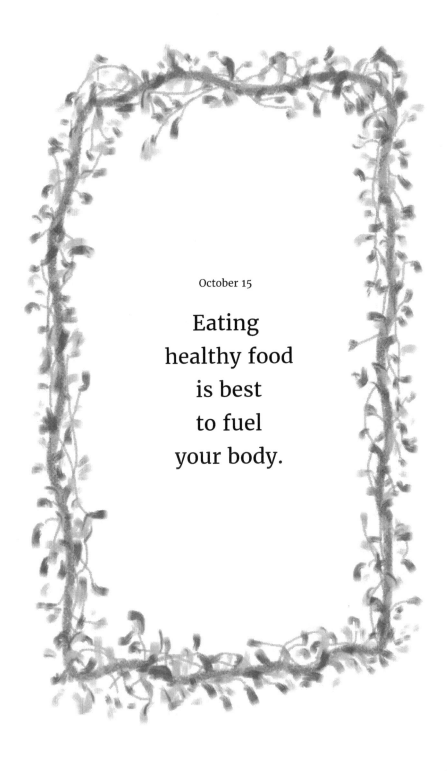

October 15

Eating
healthy food
is best
to fuel
your body.

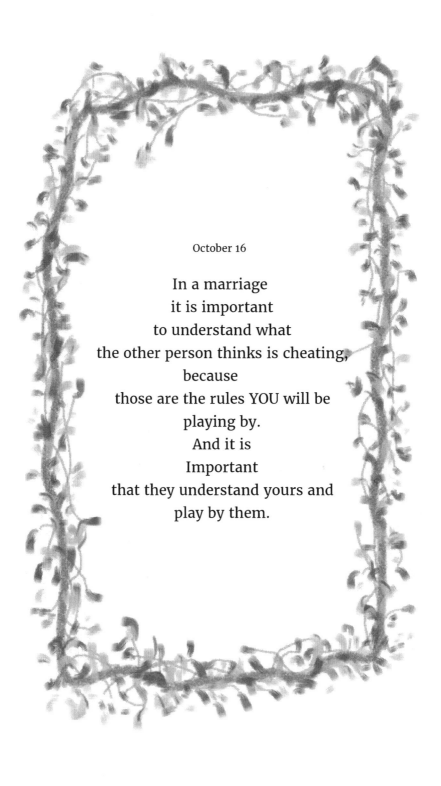

October 16

In a marriage
it is important
to understand what
the other person thinks is cheating,
because
those are the rules YOU will be
playing by.
And it is
Important
that they understand yours and
play by them.

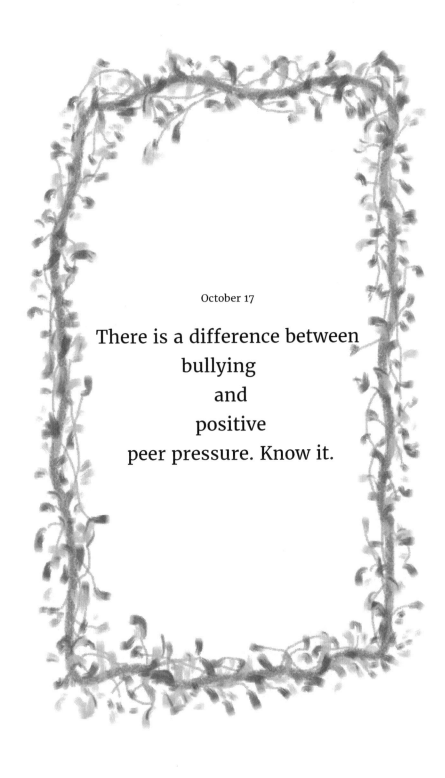

October 17

There is a difference between
bullying
and
positive
peer pressure. Know it.

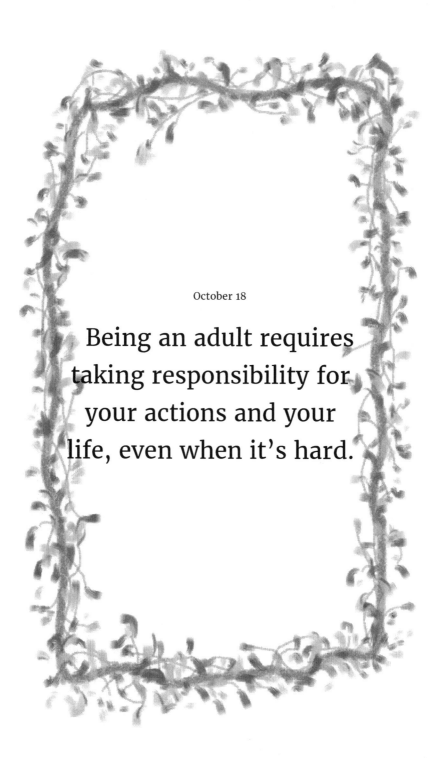

October 18

Being an adult requires taking responsibility for your actions and your life, even when it's hard.

October 19

When people
feel consistently left out
and
mistreated
and
don't think
that anyone
likes them
or cares, sometimes
they act out violently.

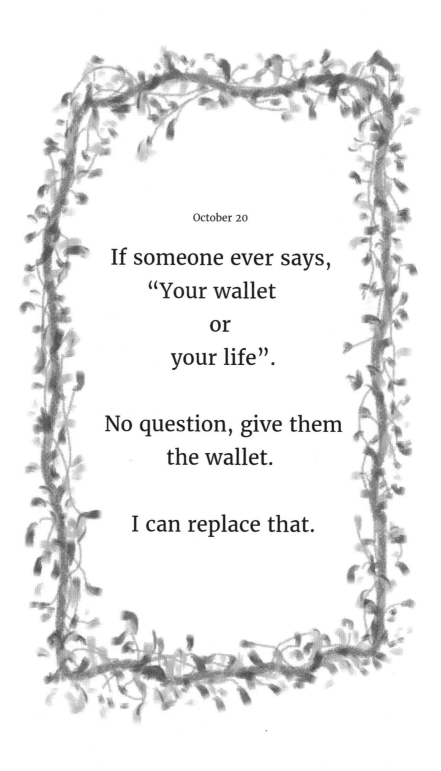

October 20

If someone ever says,
"Your wallet
or
your life".

No question, give them
the wallet.

I can replace that.

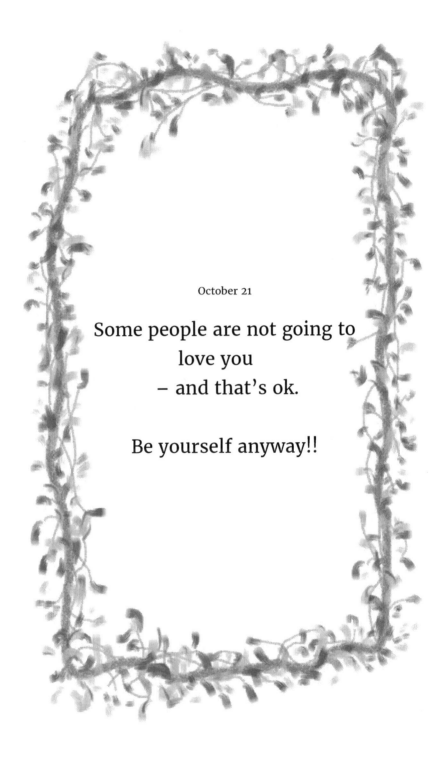

October 21

Some people are not going to
love you
– and that's ok.

Be yourself anyway!!

October 22

Secrets
can kill you.
If it feels like shame,
telling a trusted friend
or
family member can help.

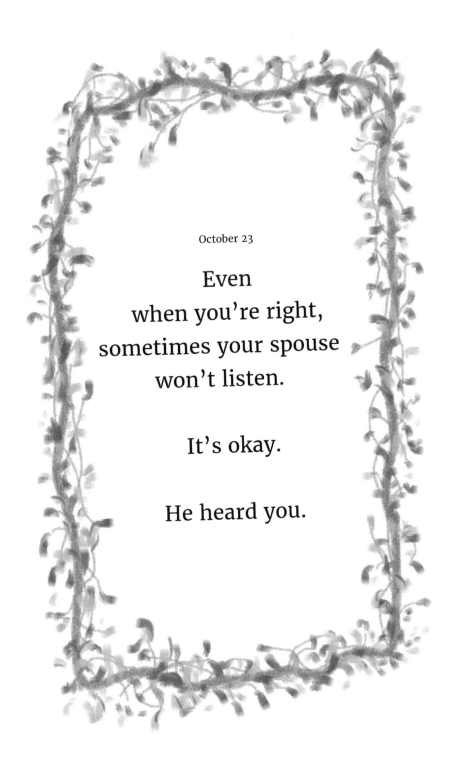

October 23

Even
when you're right,
sometimes your spouse
won't listen.

It's okay.

He heard you.

October 24

All spouses
need to be right
sometimes.

Make sure
you recognize it.

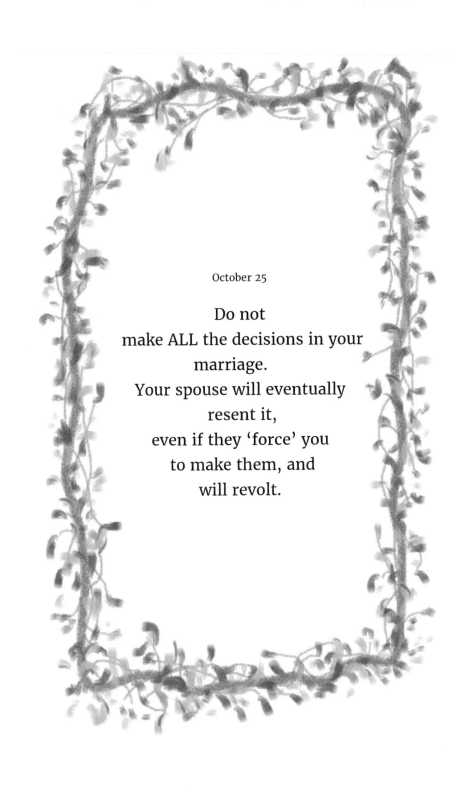

October 25

Do not
make ALL the decisions in your
marriage.
Your spouse will eventually
resent it,
even if they 'force' you
to make them, and
will revolt.

October 26

Stubbornness
is a
great power.

Use it wisely.

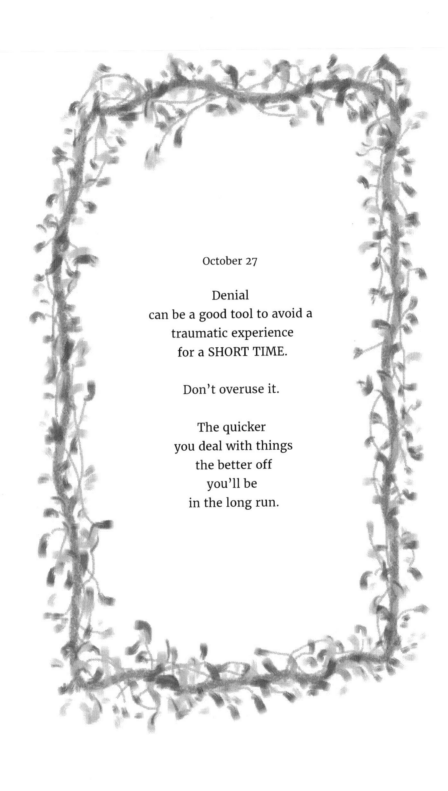

October 27

Denial
can be a good tool to avoid a
traumatic experience
for a SHORT TIME.

Don't overuse it.

The quicker
you deal with things
the better off
you'll be
in the long run.

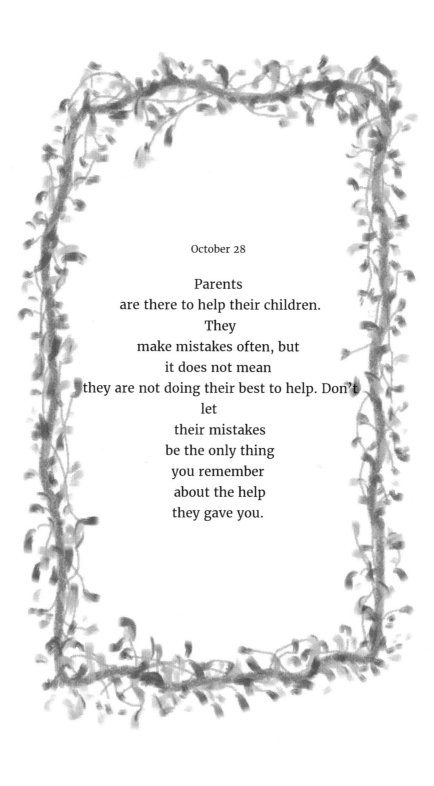

October 28

Parents
are there to help their children.
They
make mistakes often, but
it does not mean
they are not doing their best to help. Don't
let
their mistakes
be the only thing
you remember
about the help
they gave you.

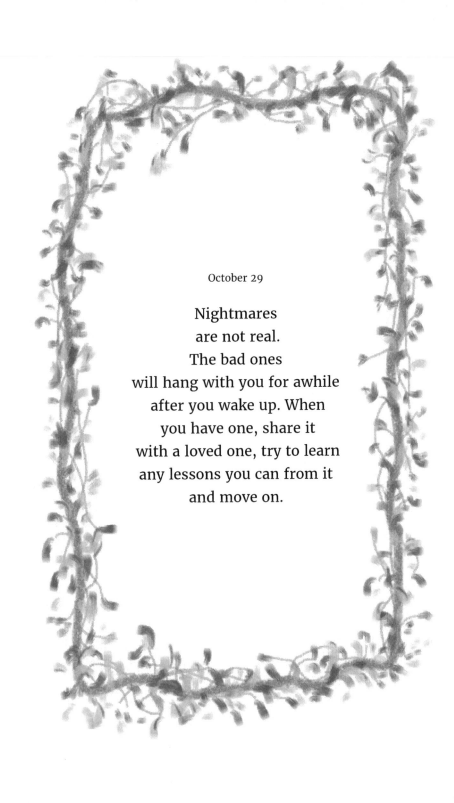

October 29

Nightmares
are not real.
The bad ones
will hang with you for awhile
after you wake up. When
you have one, share it
with a loved one, try to learn
any lessons you can from it
and move on.

October 30

When you
wake up late
for something important,
move quickly,
skip doing anything unnecessary,
brush your teeth, and
drive carefully.
It's
the best
that you can do.

October 31

If you are watching
a lot of tv
all the time,
you haven't
set your goals high
enough.

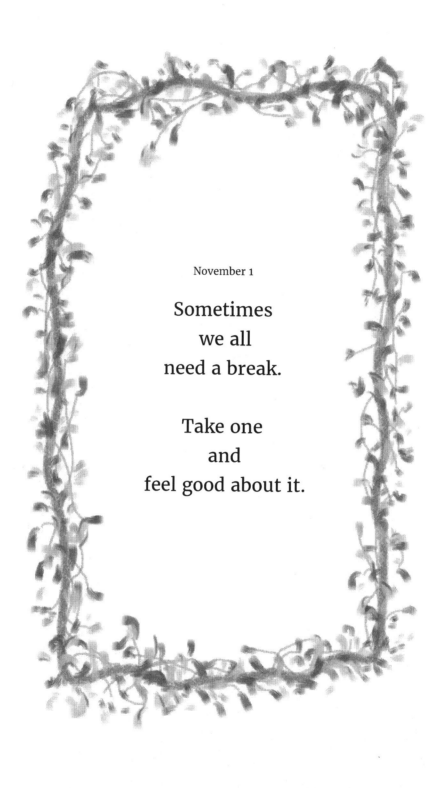

November 1

Sometimes
we all
need a break.

Take one
and
feel good about it.

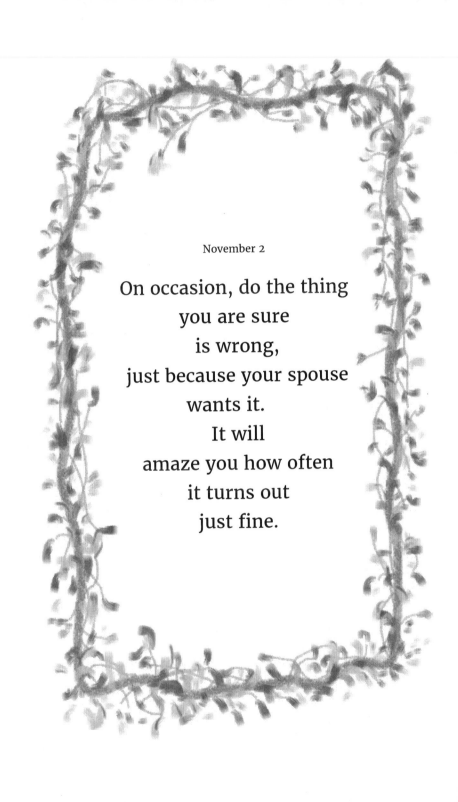

November 2

On occasion, do the thing
you are sure
is wrong,
just because your spouse
wants it.
It will
amaze you how often
it turns out
just fine.

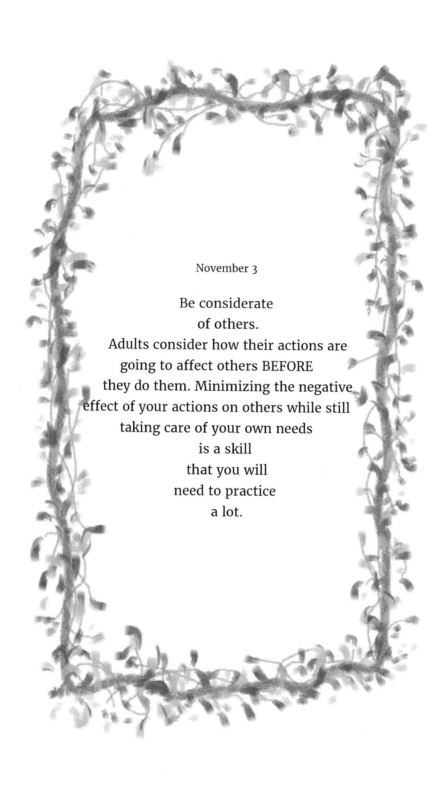

November 3

Be considerate
of others.
Adults consider how their actions are
going to affect others BEFORE
they do them. Minimizing the negative
effect of your actions on others while still
taking care of your own needs
is a skill
that you will
need to practice
a lot.

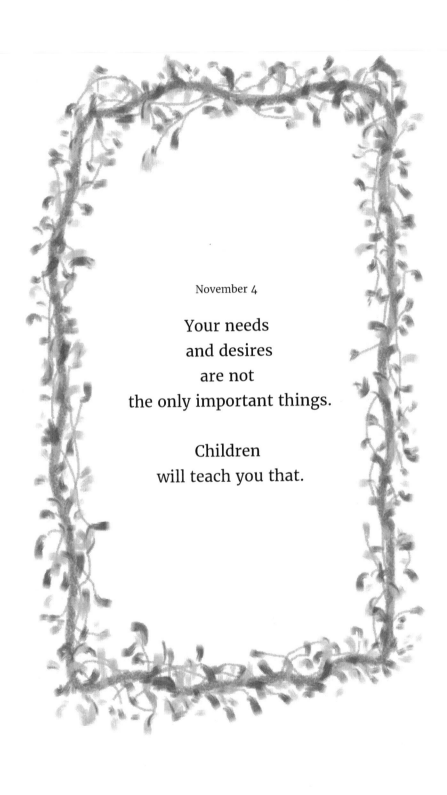

November 4

Your needs
and desires
are not
the only important things.

Children
will teach you that.

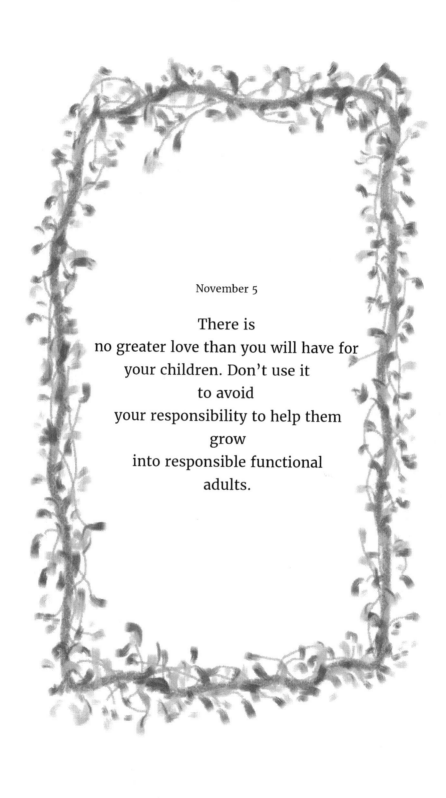

November 5

There is
no greater love than you will have for
your children. Don't use it
to avoid
your responsibility to help them
grow
into responsible functional
adults.

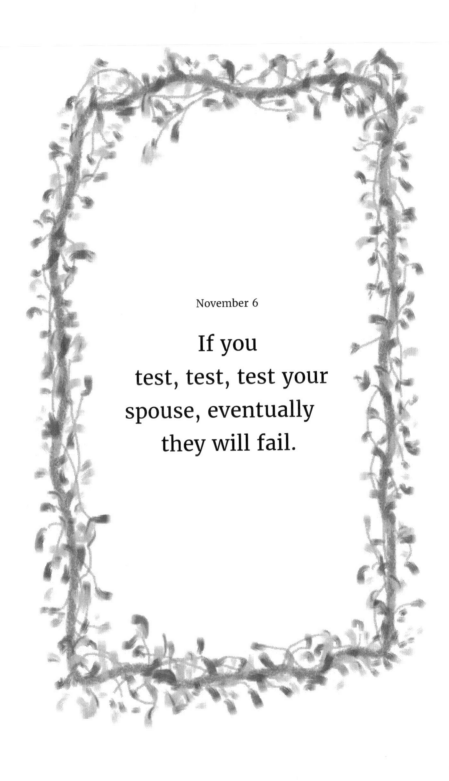

November 6

If you
test, test, test your
spouse, eventually
they will fail.

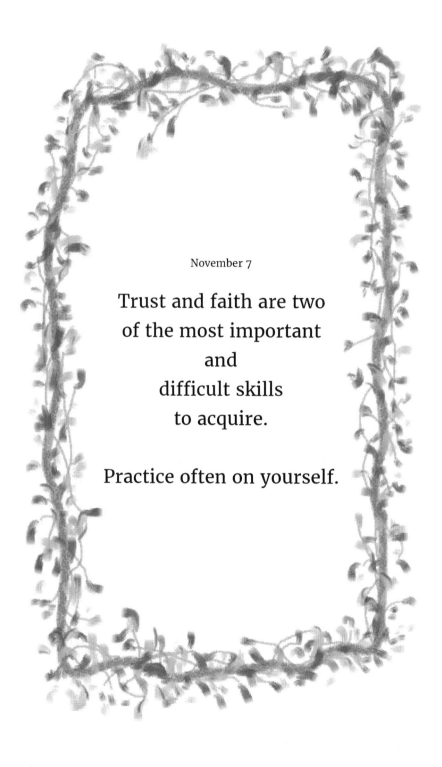

November 7

Trust and faith are two
of the most important
and
difficult skills
to acquire.

Practice often on yourself.

November 8

When there is
a tragedy,
there is always
a good consequence. Look hard.
If you
can't find it, create it.

November 9

Give
yourself
time to heal. Then
Excel.

November 10

People
act funny when
they miss you.

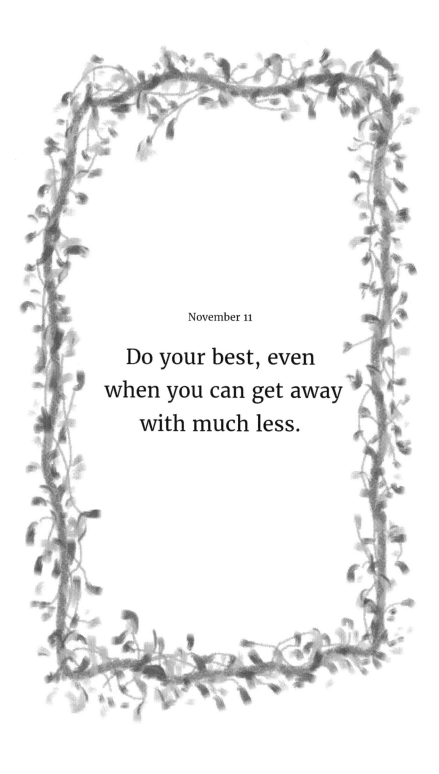

November 11

Do your best, even
when you can get away
with much less.

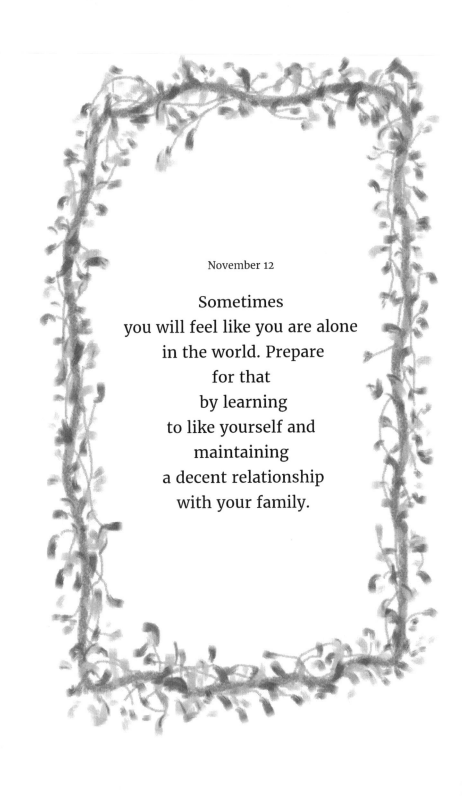

November 12

Sometimes
you will feel like you are alone
in the world. Prepare
for that
by learning
to like yourself and
maintaining
a decent relationship
with your family.

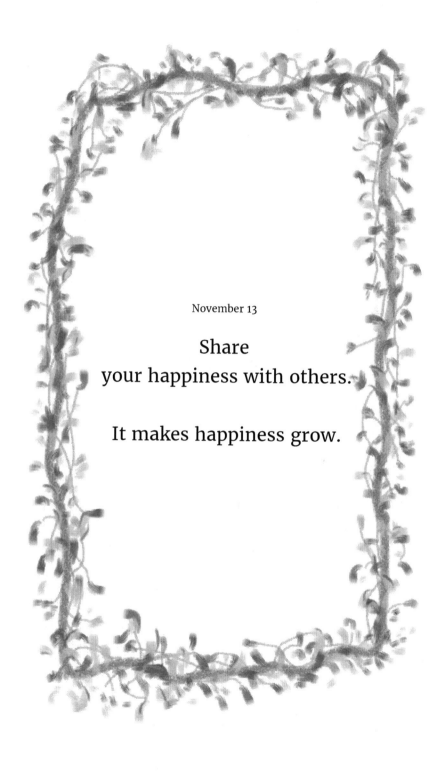

November 13

Share
your happiness with others.

It makes happiness grow.

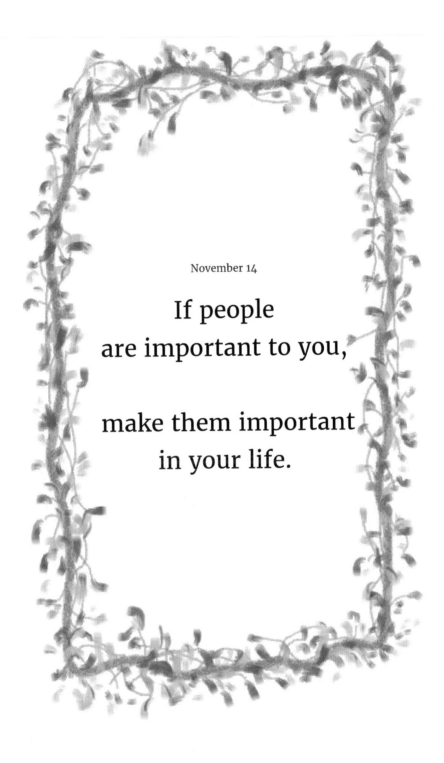

November 14

If people
are important to you,

make them important
in your life.

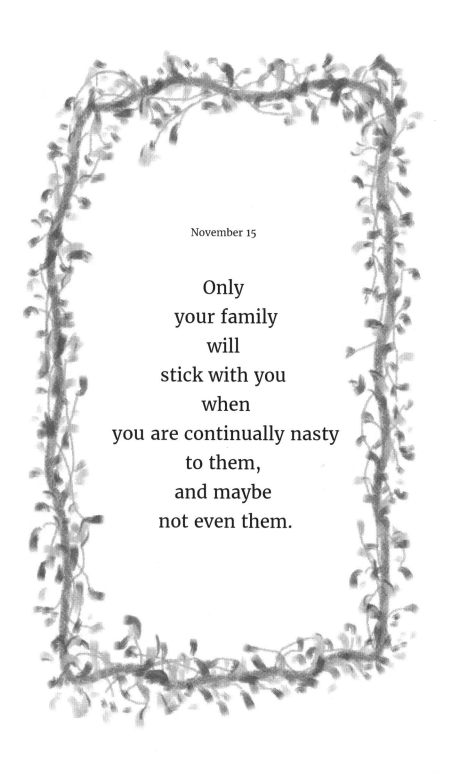

November 15

Only
your family
will
stick with you
when
you are continually nasty
to them,
and maybe
not even them.

November 16

People use sex
for a lot
of things.

The best is when
it is a joining
of two people in love.

November 17

Falling in love
is
an emotional rollercoaster
of hormones
and pheromones and is a real rush.

Loving someone is a choice,
and
sometimes
it's hard.

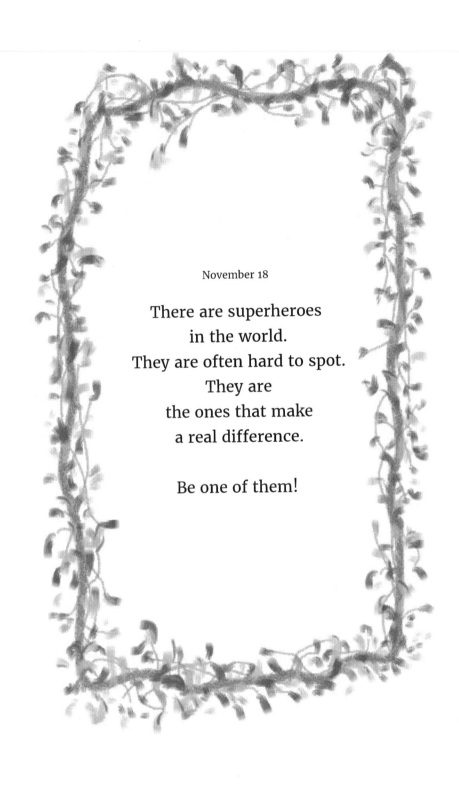

November 18

There are superheroes
in the world.
They are often hard to spot.
They are
the ones that make
a real difference.

Be one of them!

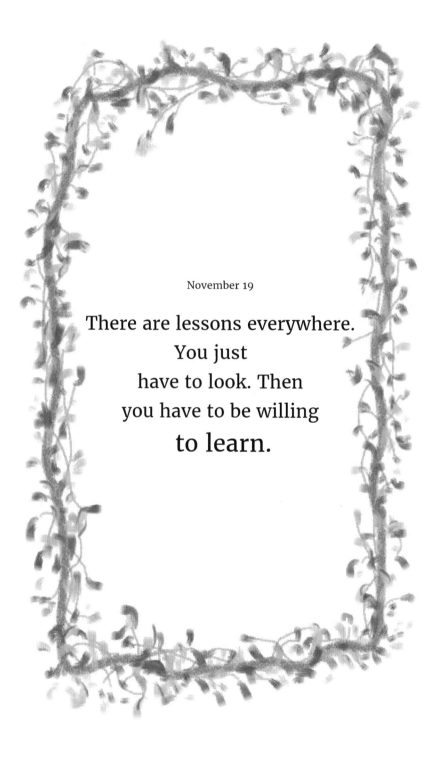

November 19

There are lessons everywhere.
You just
have to look. Then
you have to be willing
to learn.

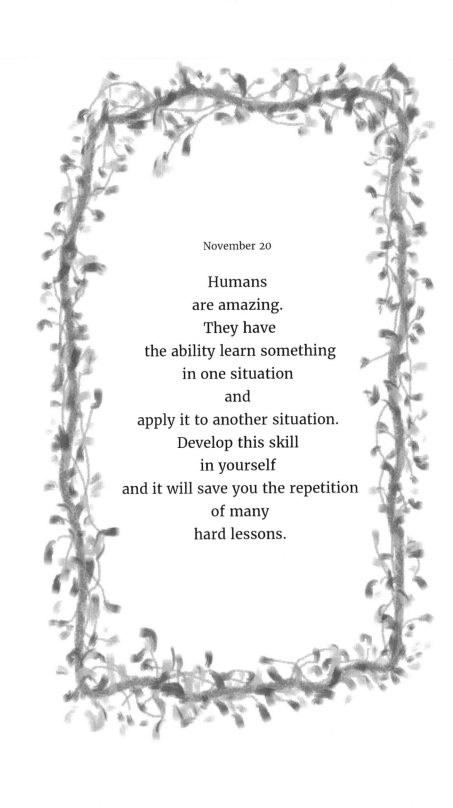

November 20

Humans
are amazing.
They have
the ability learn something
in one situation
and
apply it to another situation.
Develop this skill
in yourself
and it will save you the repetition
of many
hard lessons.

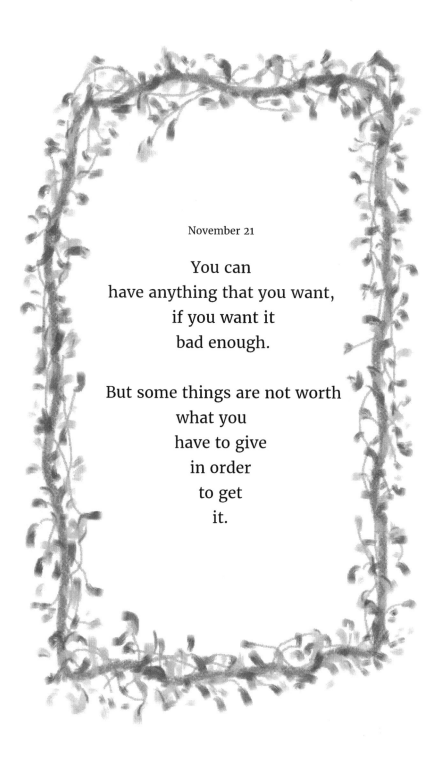

November 21

You can
have anything that you want,
if you want it
bad enough.

But some things are not worth
what you
have to give
in order
to get
it.

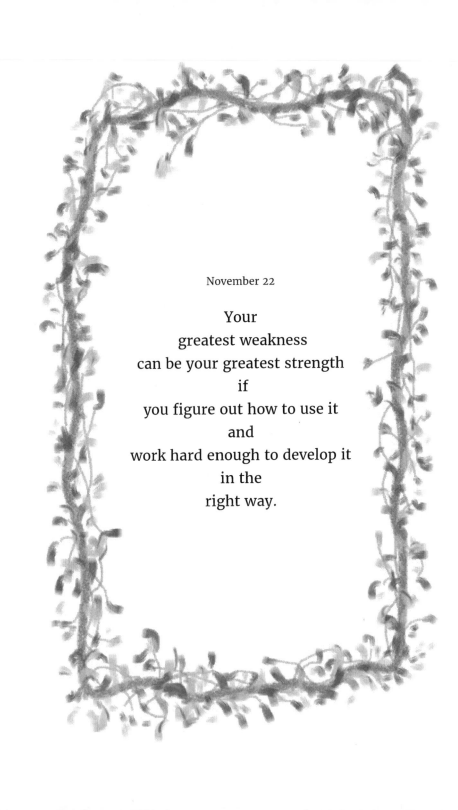

November 22

Your
greatest weakness
can be your greatest strength
if
you figure out how to use it
and
work hard enough to develop it
in the
right way.

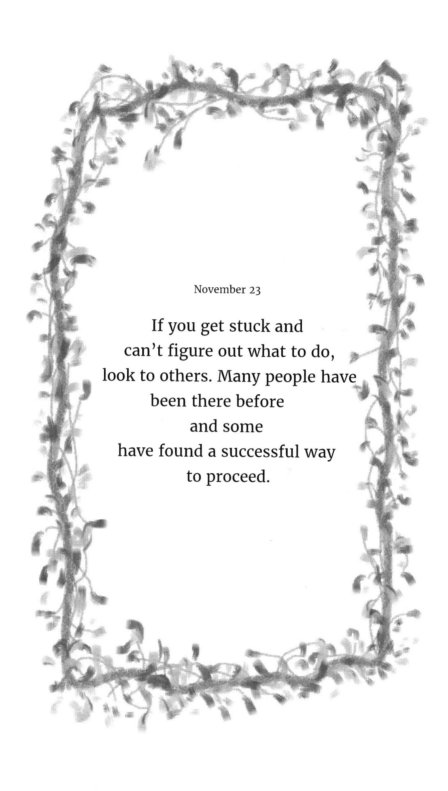

November 23

If you get stuck and
can't figure out what to do,
look to others. Many people have
been there before
and some
have found a successful way
to proceed.

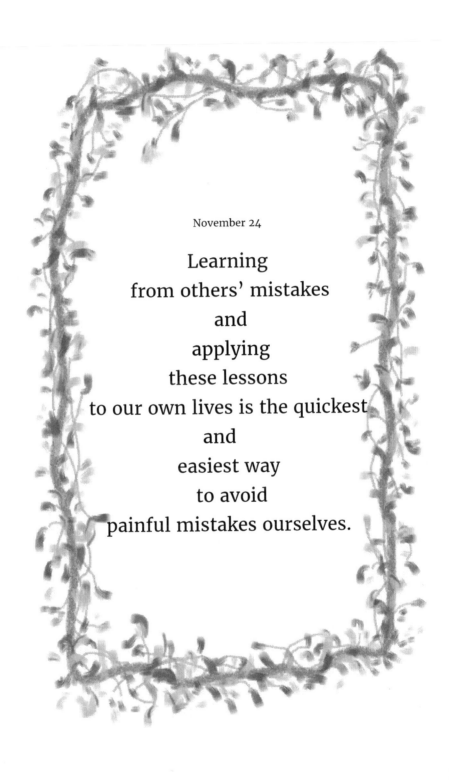

November 24

Learning
from others' mistakes
and
applying
these lessons
to our own lives is the quickest
and
easiest way
to avoid
painful mistakes ourselves.

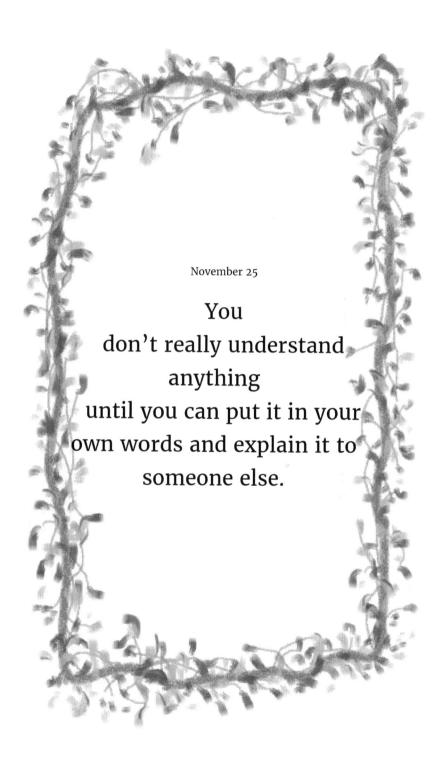

November 25

You
don't really understand
anything
until you can put it in your
own words and explain it to
someone else.

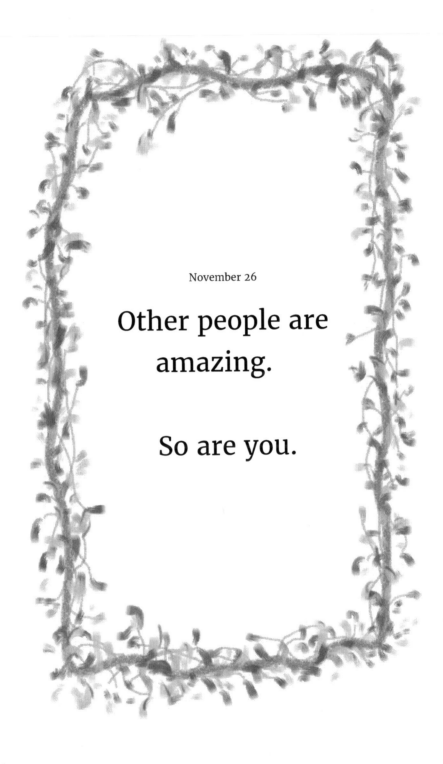

November 26

Other people are amazing.

So are you.

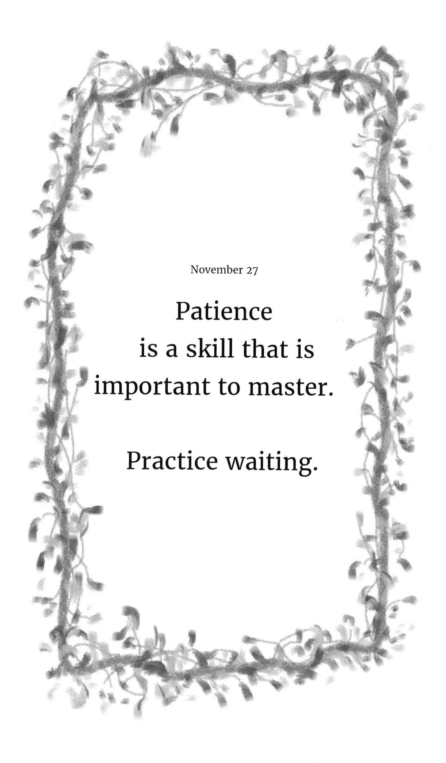

November 27

Patience
is a skill that is
important to master.

Practice waiting.

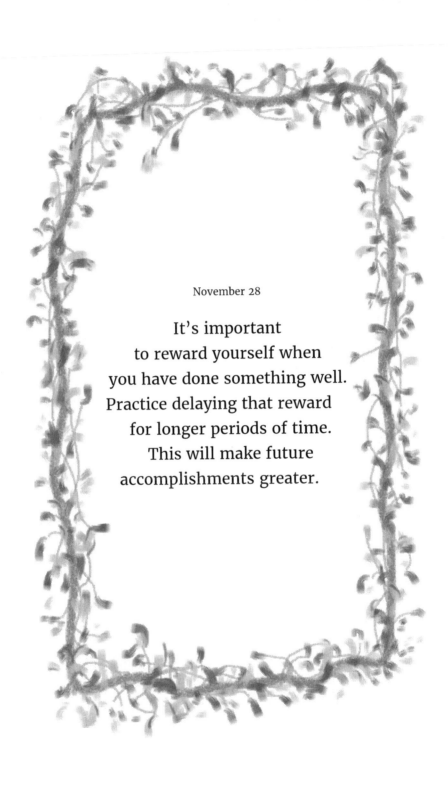

November 28

It's important
to reward yourself when
you have done something well.
Practice delaying that reward
for longer periods of time.
This will make future
accomplishments greater.

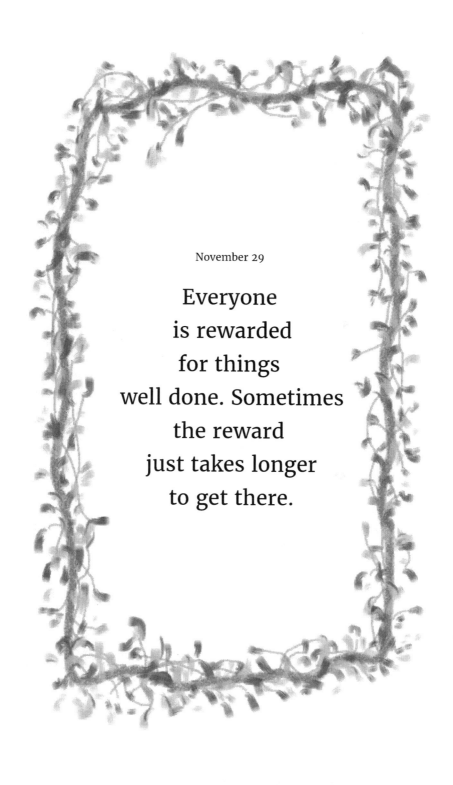

November 29

Everyone
is rewarded
for things
well done. Sometimes
the reward
just takes longer
to get there.

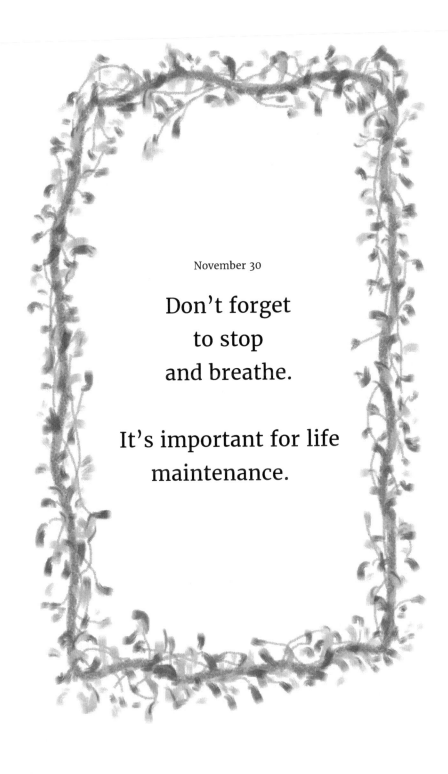

November 30

Don't forget
to stop
and breathe.

It's important for life
maintenance.

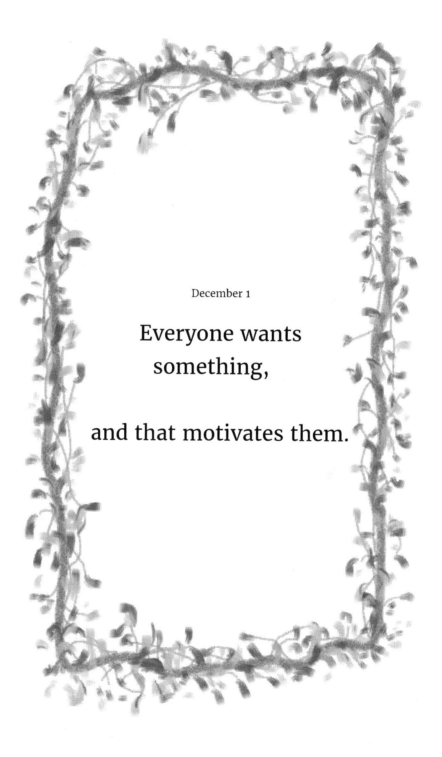

December 1

Everyone wants
something,

and that motivates them.

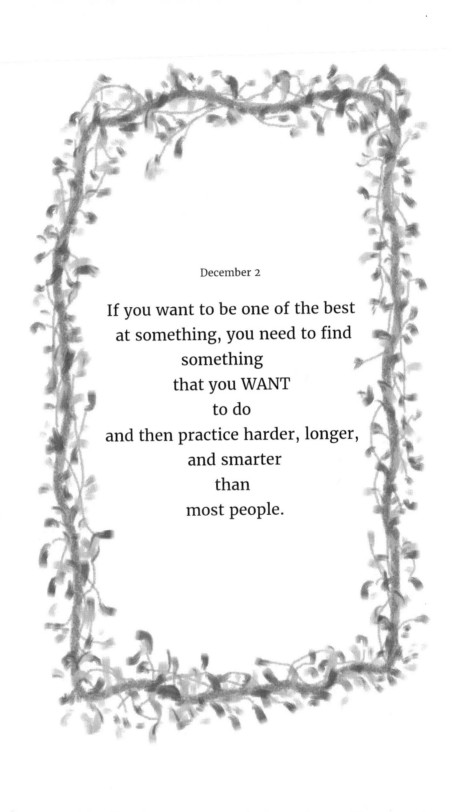

December 2

If you want to be one of the best
at something, you need to find
something
that you WANT
to do
and then practice harder, longer,
and smarter
than
most people.

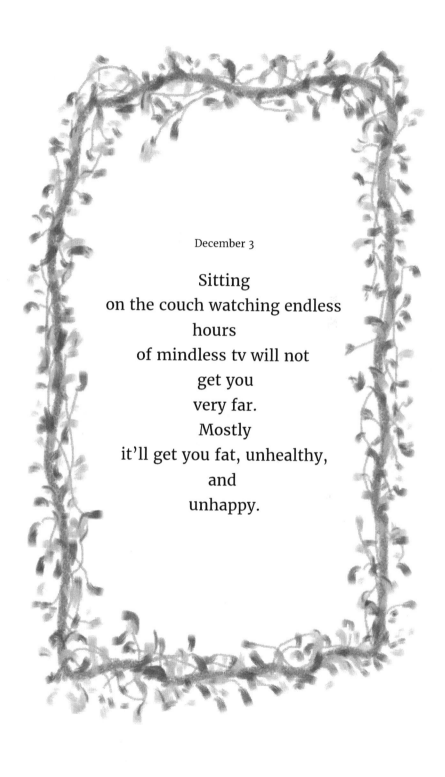

December 3

Sitting
on the couch watching endless
hours
of mindless tv will not
get you
very far.
Mostly
it'll get you fat, unhealthy,
and
unhappy.

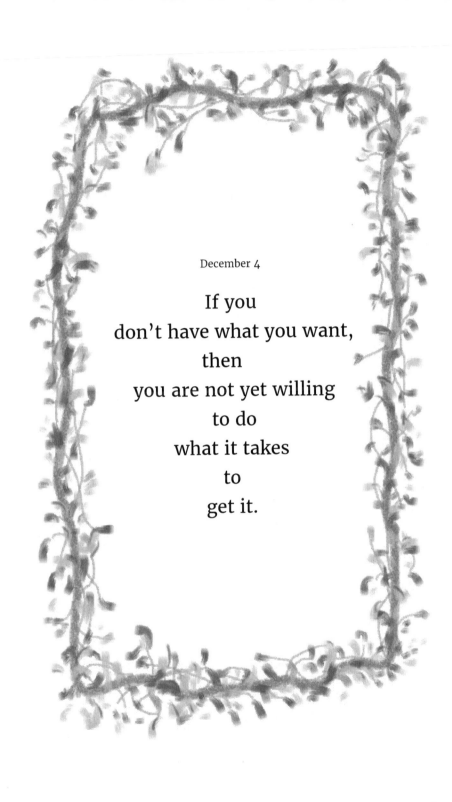

December 4

If you
don't have what you want,
then
you are not yet willing
to do
what it takes
to
get it.

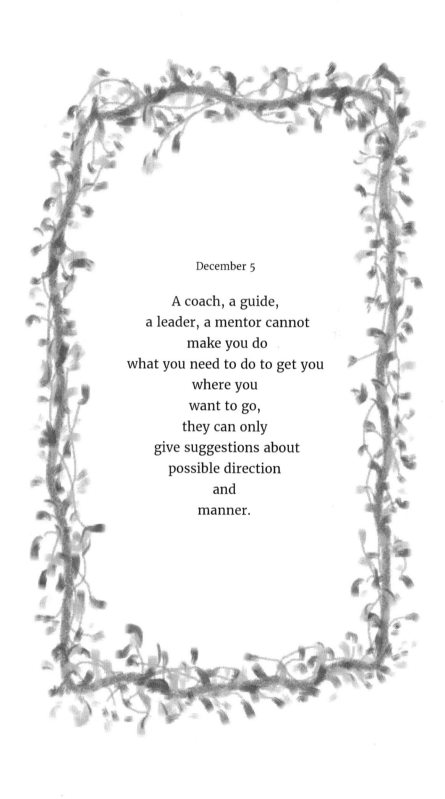

December 5

A coach, a guide,
a leader, a mentor cannot
make you do
what you need to do to get you
where you
want to go,
they can only
give suggestions about
possible direction
and
manner.

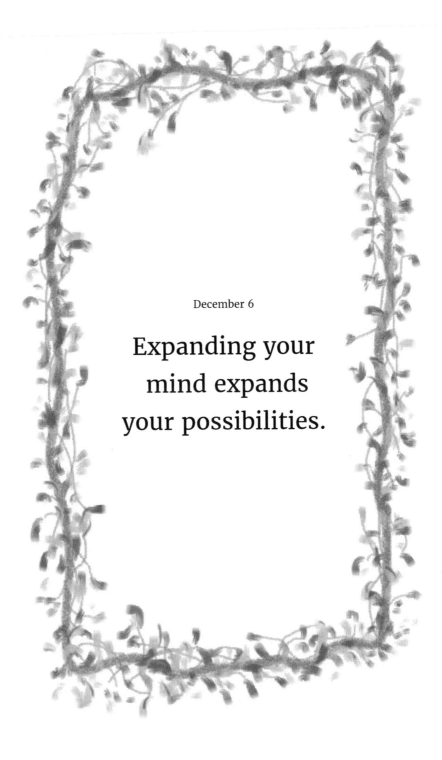

December 6

Expanding your mind expands your possibilities.

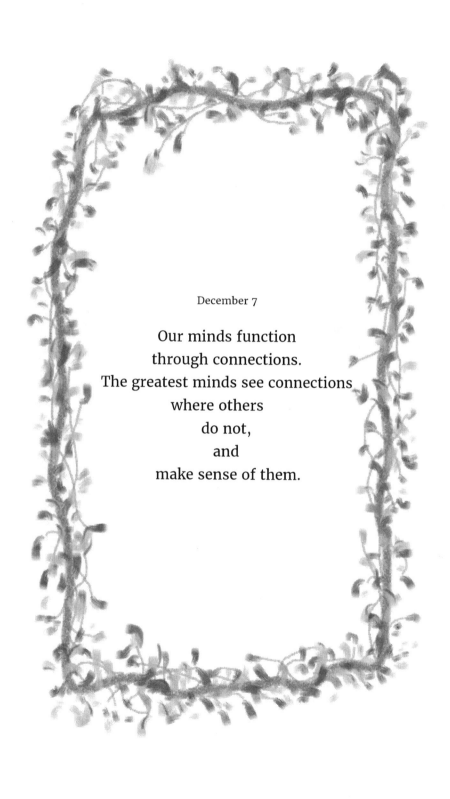

December 7

Our minds function
through connections.
The greatest minds see connections
where others
do not,
and
make sense of them.

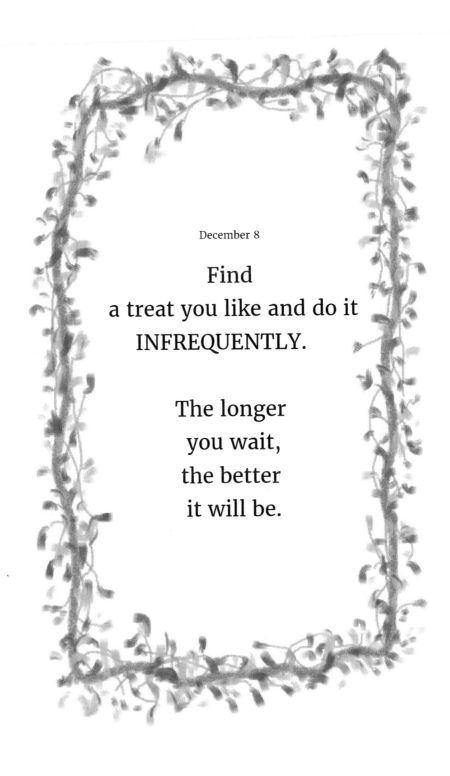

December 8

Find
a treat you like and do it
INFREQUENTLY.

The longer
you wait,
the better
it will be.

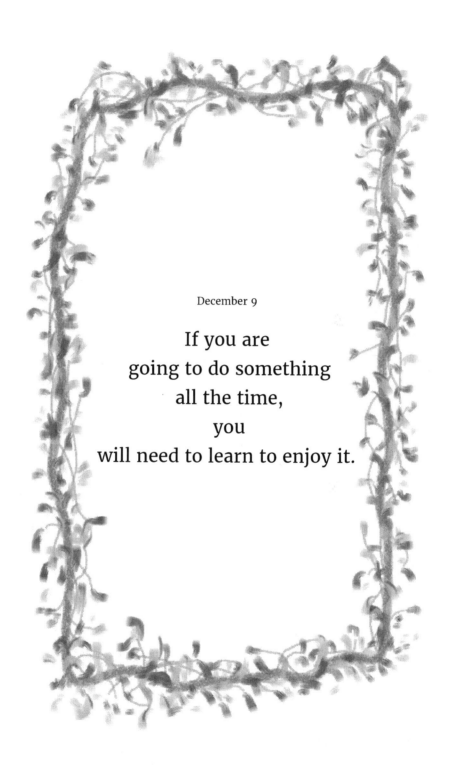

December 9

If you are
going to do something
all the time,
you
will need to learn to enjoy it.

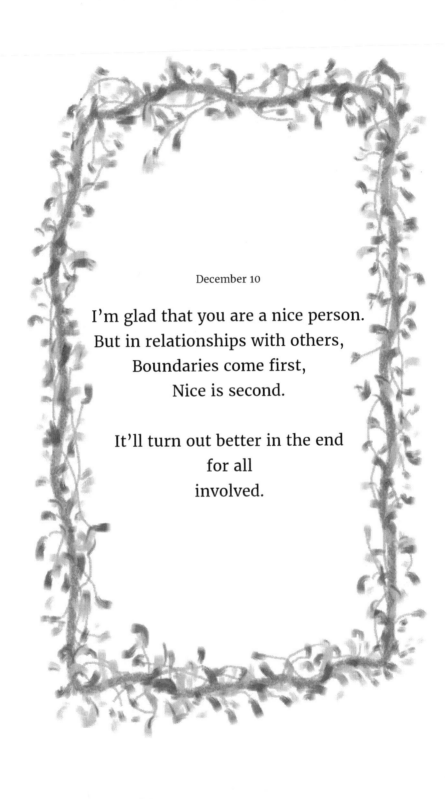

December 10

I'm glad that you are a nice person.
But in relationships with others,
Boundaries come first,
Nice is second.

It'll turn out better in the end
for all
involved.

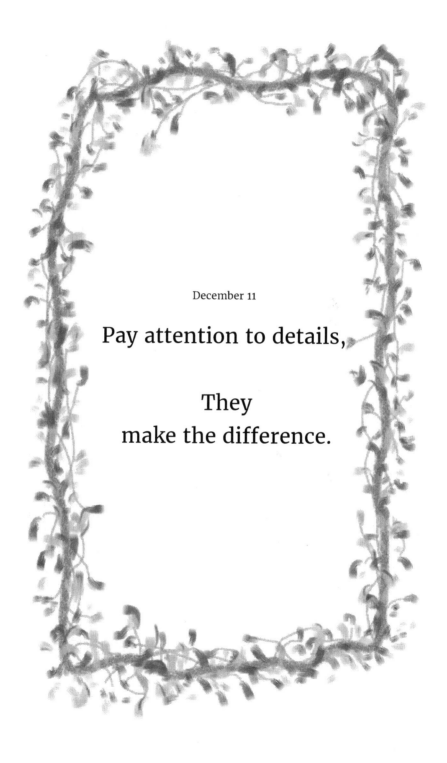

December 11

Pay attention to details,

They
make the difference.

December 12

When
you get married, TWO
do not become ONE PERSON, they
become ONE TEAM.
Work together.

December 13

The best
that you can do
is
THE BEST THAT YOU CAN DO!

Let that be enough.

December 14

Sometimes anger
is used
to mask hurt
or fear. Recognize it
in yourself
and
others.

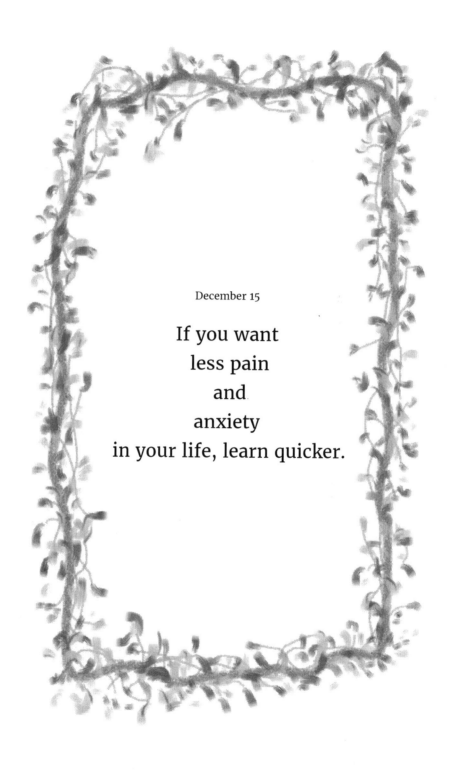

December 15

If you want
less pain
and
anxiety
in your life, learn quicker.

December 16

Change
is hard...
but it can also be good.

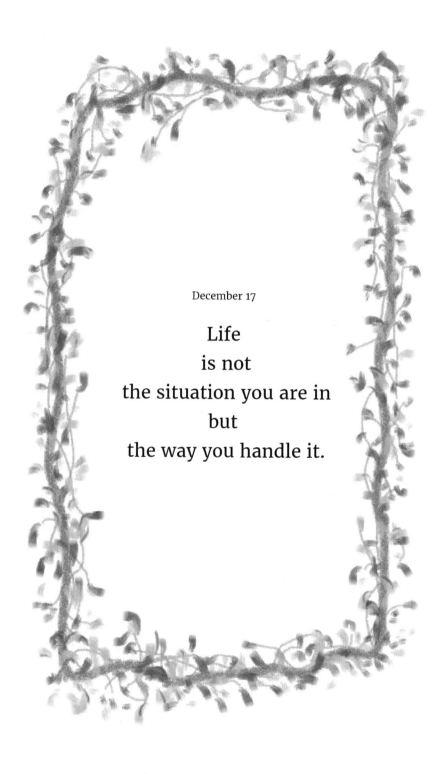

December 17

Life
is not
the situation you are in
but
the way you handle it.

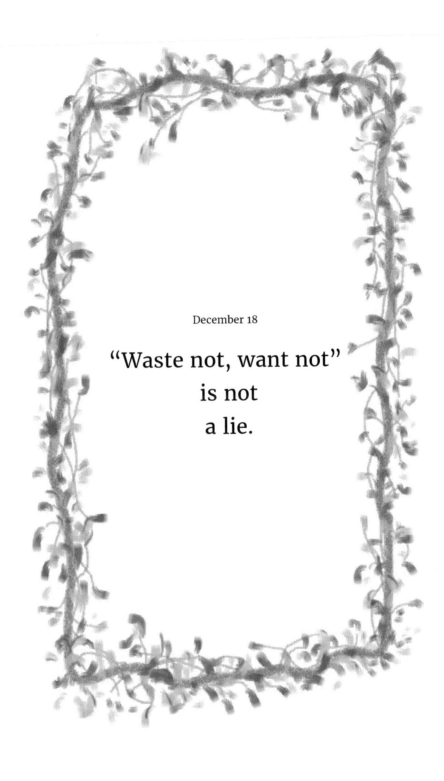

December 18

"Waste not, want not"
is not
a lie.

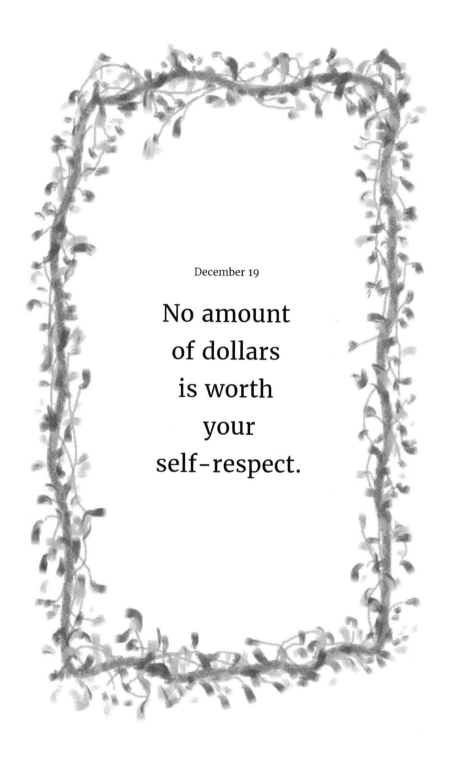

December 19

No amount of dollars is worth your self-respect.

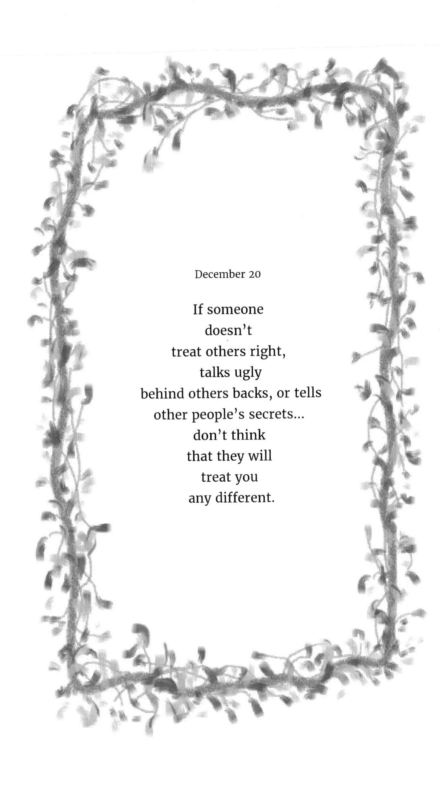

December 20

If someone
doesn't
treat others right,
talks ugly
behind others backs, or tells
other people's secrets...
don't think
that they will
treat you
any different.

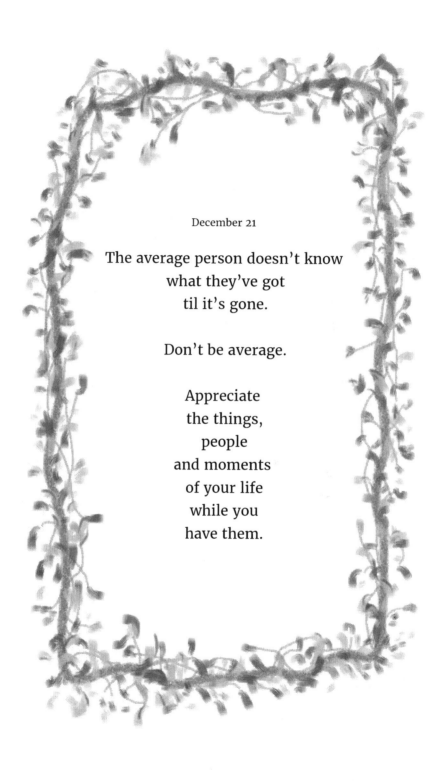

December 21

The average person doesn't know
what they've got
til it's gone.

Don't be average.

Appreciate
the things,
people
and moments
of your life
while you
have them.

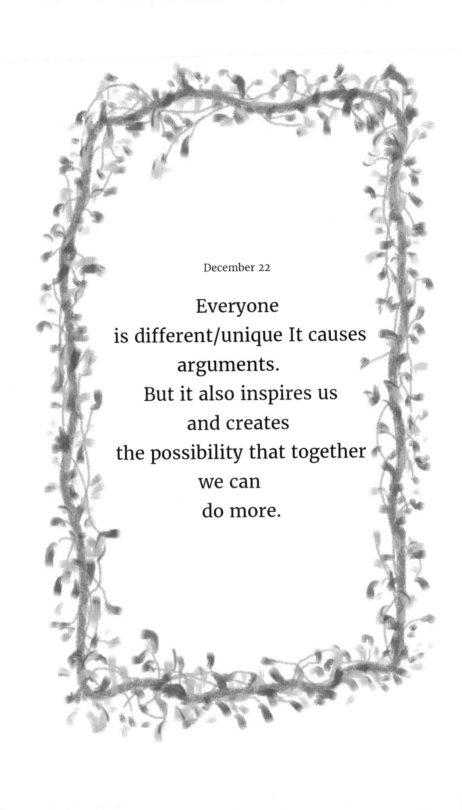

December 22

Everyone
is different/unique It causes
arguments.
But it also inspires us
and creates
the possibility that together
we can
do more.

December 23

Every
good day
must come
to an end,
just like
every bad day must come
to an end.

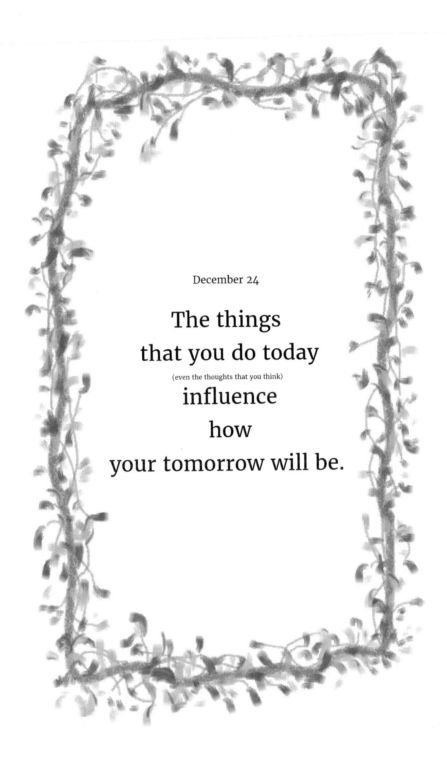

December 24

The things
that you do today

(even the thoughts that you think)

influence

how

your tomorrow will be.

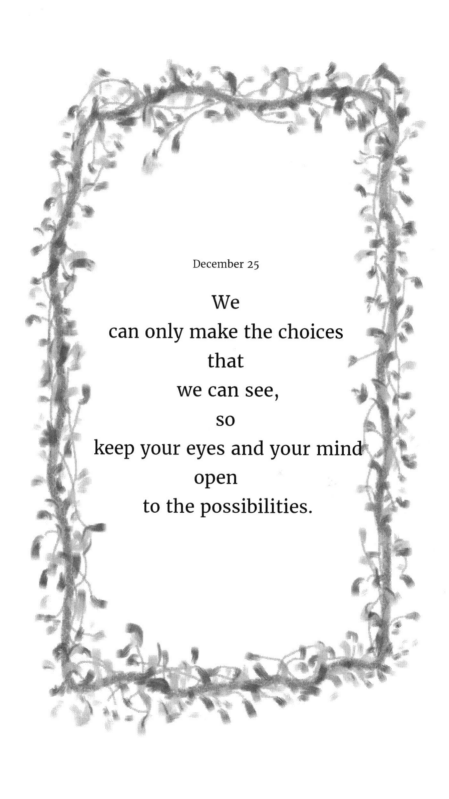

December 25

We
can only make the choices
that
we can see,
so
keep your eyes and your mind
open
to the possibilities.

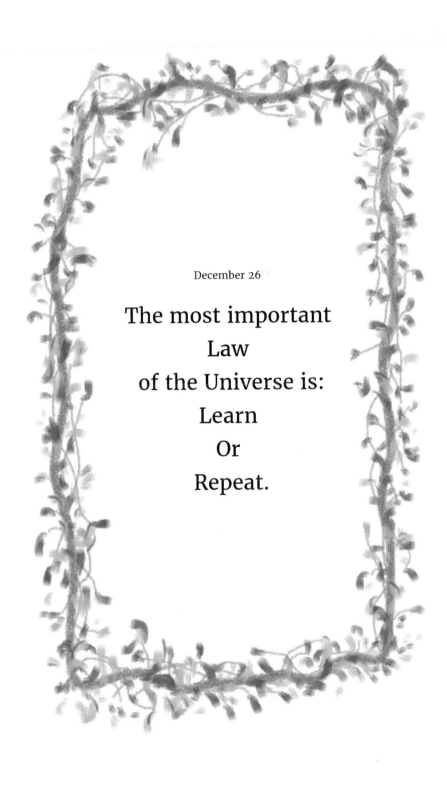

December 26

The most important
Law
of the Universe is:
Learn
Or
Repeat.

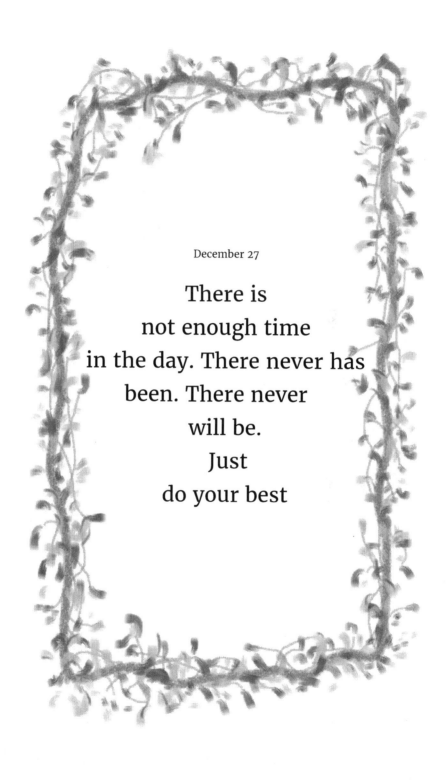

December 27

There is
not enough time
in the day. There never has
been. There never
will be.
Just
do your best

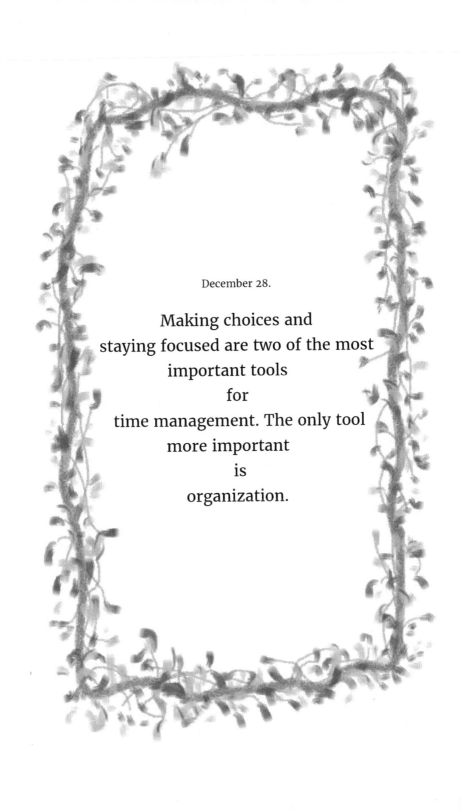

December 28.

Making choices and
staying focused are two of the most
important tools
for
time management. The only tool
more important
is
organization.

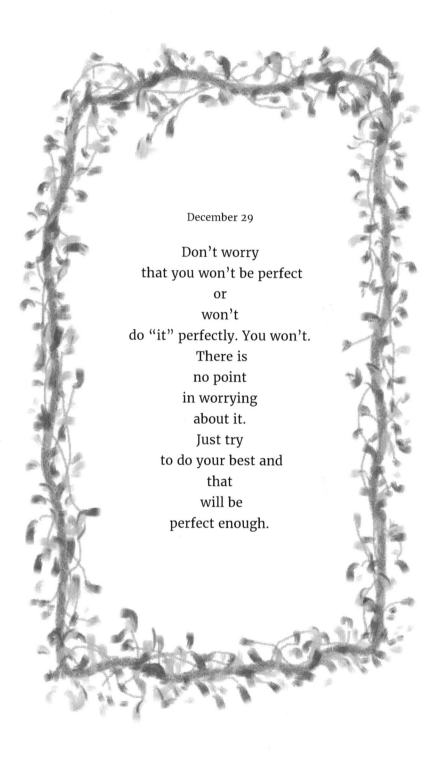

December 29

Don't worry
that you won't be perfect
or
won't
do "it" perfectly. You won't.
There is
no point
in worrying
about it.
Just try
to do your best and
that
will be
perfect enough.

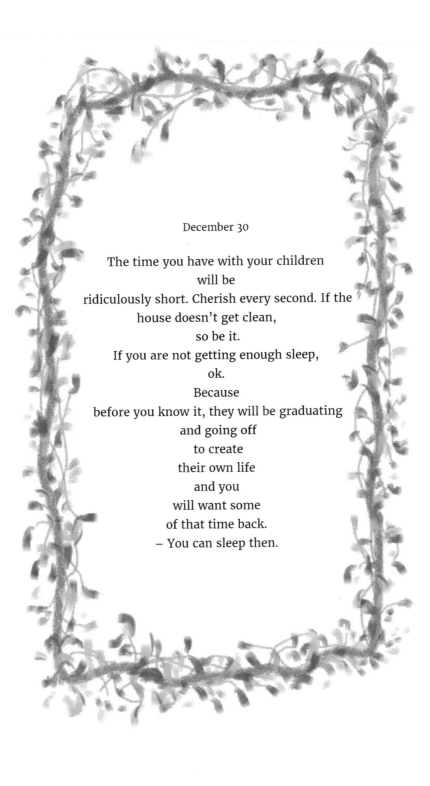

December 30

The time you have with your children
will be
ridiculously short. Cherish every second. If the
house doesn't get clean,
so be it.
If you are not getting enough sleep,
ok.
Because
before you know it, they will be graduating
and going off
to create
their own life
and you
will want some
of that time back.
– You can sleep then.

December 31
You
will NOT BELIEVE how strongly
you love
your children. When
they come
into your life,
you will question whether
you ever
knew what
the word
LOVE meant before you saw them.

Mwaaa!

Love you once,
Love you twice,
Love you More
Than a Hog
Loves rice!!
forever
&
always Sunshine

Made in the USA
San Bernardino, CA
13 May 2019